The Social Domain in CSR and Sustainability

Dr Thiel's The Social Domain in CSR and Sustainability *analyzes the extensive research for CSR and provides an important new study that makes insightful contributions to the Corporate Social Responsibility (CSR) literature, especially for practitioners and researchers who are seeking to understand the meanings of CSR among diverse constituents and institutions. Most organizations operate in the complex "social domains" described by Dr Thiel, but unfortunately many of them fail to recognize both the scope and complexity of achieving and communicating "social responsibilities". With the growing urgency of many sustainability issues around the globe, this book's critical examination of the many CSR relationships will be a welcome addition for many executive development programs, analytical studies and future research projects.*

John Grant, Visiting Fellow, Colorado State University, USA

This book is dedicated to employees worldwide in business, government and local communities that strive to better understand their role and impacts in society, and foster social, economic and environmental progress.

The Social Domain in CSR and Sustainability

A Critical Study of Social Responsibility among Governments, Local Communities and Corporations

MONICA THIEL

Routledge
Taylor & Francis Group

LONDON AND NEW YORK

First published 2015 by Gower Publishing

2 Park Square, Milton Park, Abingdon, Oxfordshire OX14 4RN
52 Vanderbilt Avenue, New York, NY 10017

Routledge is an imprint of the Taylor & Francis Group, an informa business

First issued in paperback 2019

Gower Applied Business Research
Our programme provides leaders, practitioners, scholars and researchers with thought provoking, cutting edge books that combine conceptual insights, interdisciplinary rigour and practical relevance in key areas of business and management.

British Library Cataloguing in Publication Data
A catalogue record for this book is available from the British Library.

Library of Congress Cataloging-in-Publication Data
Thiel, Monica, 1962-
    The social domain in CSR and sustainability : a critical study of social responsibility among governments, local communities and corporations / by Monica Thiel.
        pages cm
    Includes bibliographical references and index.
        ISBN 978-1-4724-5637-3 (hardback)
    1. Social responsibility of business. 2. Business ethics. 3. Social participation.
        I. Title.
    HD60.T4756 2015
    658.4'08--dc23

2015012432

ISBN 978-1-4724-5637-3 (hbk)
ISBN 978-0-367-88071-2 (pbk)

Contents

Contents

List of Figures

List of Tables

Preface

Very little is published about the social domain within corporate social responsibility and sustainability among corporations, governments and local communities. This book examines the factors that lead to an under-developed social domain in CSR and sustainability and how this impacts local communities' reciprocation in social responsibility to corporations. Furthermore, examination and discussion of local communities' impacts on local, regional, national and global competitiveness, sustains questionable societal values, unrealistic societal expectations and decreases social progress due to a void of critical social and personal development that is crucial for increasing social responsibility among local communities, governments and corporations.

This book is meant to help local communities, corporations and governments to identify and manage challenges and gaps of social responsibility in CSR and sustainability and to establish greater understanding of the role of society within multiple realities of CSR and sustainability. Some of the big and meaningful questions that this book answers are:

a) How can greater understanding of social responsibility within local communities empower companies, local communities and governments?

b) What are the characteristics of the manager that integrates qualitative and quantitative social domain strategies and performance successfully worldwide?

c) What is the relationship among business, local communities and governments within social responsibility in developing, emerging and advanced economies?

d) What is the nature of the relationship between individual responsibility, social responsibility and profit?

e) What is the responsibility scope and challenges of CSR and sustainability in business, governments and local communities?

f) How can companies, local communities and governments succeed in CSR and sustainability?

Intended Audience

This book is designated as a learning tool for MBA and MPP/MPA programs in universities and colleges in the academic sector. In addition, the book provides practical tools for business, government and local community leaders that are faced with challenging societal constraints and consumer and public demands on a daily basis from differing cultures, sectors and industries. Readers of this book will be in a better position to manage and develop CSR and sustainability strategies and initiatives worldwide.

Overview of Book

This book begins with an introduction to establish how current dimensions of the social domain in CSR and sustainability are overlapping and separated within business, society and government. Chapter 1 discusses how society co-creates and drives social responsibility in corporations and governments worldwide with discussion of societal values and beliefs, trust, competitiveness and expectations within CSR and sustainability.

Chapter 2 examines six constituents of social domain fragmentation deriving from current theories, methodologies and definitions. In Chapter 3, human bias and fragmentation in social responsibility derived from competing cultural, discipline, knowledge preferences and social environments among local communities, governments and corporations provides the reader with seven specific CSR and sustainability fragmentation challenges. Further discussion will include how societal competitiveness can determine society's potential impact on local, regional, national and global competitive advantage in CSR and sustainability. Chapter 4 will discuss how governments, corporations and local communities impact each other in CSR and sustainability with an examination of personal trust and individual accomplishment in CSR and sustainability. A social responsibility model created by the author is introduced as a way to manage tensions between relational risk and the common good. The final chapter, Chapter 5, includes recommendations and potential outcomes for corporations and governments working with local communities in CSR and sustainability initiatives and projects. Social domain strategies of well-known corporations are discussed for business, governance and societal relevance, competitiveness and problem formulation in a global volatile economy. In addition, recommendations and potential outcomes for governments include examination of societal competitiveness beyond economic, technological and societal well-being, positive and negative effects of social cohesion, and differing local community mindsets for local, regional, national and global competitive advantage.

Acknowledgments

In a world where societal well-being indicators and measurements determine and define what is a healthy society and governments create and implement regulations and social policies, businesses face unique and deep challenges of managing, leveraging and engaging multiple human and social values and social identities to expand and sustain social responsibility within operations worldwide. I am deeply grateful to the practitioners in companies and governments that participated in this study and for their unending pursuit to innovate and create economic, environmental and social progress.

About the Author

Doctor Monica Thiel is a member of the Academy of Management and the European Group for Organizational Studies. Her research articles and case studies have been published in the *American Journal of Economics and Business Administration*, *International Journal of Business and Globalization*, *Asian Journal of Business and Management Cases*, *Procedia: Social and Behavioral Sciences*, and the *International Journal of Entrepreneurship and Innovation*. Prior to her pursuit of a PhD in Social Science at the Tilburg School of Social and Behavioral Sciences, she worked in multinational corporations, non-profit organizations, government, military and small–medium enterprises in business management and social responsibility initiatives. Her current research interests include corporate social responsibility, sustainability, competitiveness, strategic management and innovation.

Locating the Social Domain in Corporate Social Responsibility and Sustainability

Defining the Social Domain

There are many social domain definitions and social domain practices within corporate social responsibility (CSR) and sustainability among governments, corporations and local communities. Current dimensions of the social domain in CSR and sustainability are overlapping and separated. The construct of the social domain is measured separately and integrated within preconstructed theoretical models of CSR and sustainability. There has not been much reconstruction of the social domain, as this would require a dramatic shift institutionally across disciplines worldwide. Thus, locating the social domain in CSR and sustainability requires examining CSR and sustainability discipline boundaries for greater meanings and sense making of the social domain (Gergen and Gergen, 2008).

The social domain is the least discussed and developed in comparison to the environmental and economic domains (Opp and Saunders, 2013). Furthermore, it is important to note that differing global social values and societal beliefs promote broad variance of CSR and sustainability. In addition, an undeveloped understanding and practice of CSR and sustainability within emerging and developing countries generates a lack of solid global understanding of the social domain's impact among corporations, local communities and governments worldwide. The social domain can be viewed and defined as a continual and changing strategy among people and not just the interactions of a group of people or two or more individuals. For example, analyzing and measuring national social progress based upon socio-economic impacts and outcomes without acknowledging other impacts and outcomes from citizens may lead to social responsibility as pretense and decreasing national competitiveness. Furthermore, by overlooking alternative social impacts and sustaining overconfidence in economics to advance society can limit society's potential role and impact in generating societal progress.

The current understanding and practice of the social domain in CSR and sustainability encompasses many different pre-existing social categories found within a variety of disciplines and include topics such as socio-economics, well-being, happiness, education, global inequality, poverty, civic engagement, crime, governance, living standards, philanthropy, supply-chain management, customer satisfaction, labor relations, working conditions, wages and employment, health and safety, diversity and inclusion, human rights, child labor, societal taxes, employee relations, equal opportunity, social entrepreneurship, social integration, social innovation and co-determination. Unmet social needs and social issues demanded by activists and NGOs are placed into the social domain of CSR and sustainability. Consequently, the use of pre-existing social categories results in not developing and bringing stronger accountability to the role of people in the social domain of CSR and sustainability. Instead, it is simply sustaining social welfare.

The Significance and Impact of the Social Domain

Why is the definition of the social domain in CSR and sustainability important?

It may appear to some readers that the author is constructing the social domain in CSR and sustainability as something larger than it currently is portrayed in global reporting tools. However, current CSR and sustainability constructs have significant consequences for society because differing societal movements and institutions direct and shape social change within CSR and sustainability and could misdiagnose the positive and negative social network mechanisms and impacts. Furthermore, the social domain within CSR and sustainability can be viewed and defined as a constant micro and macro strategy between individuals and society to shape and direct relationships and partnerships among governments, local communities and corporations. For instance, examining social progress based upon societal well-being and happiness without acknowledging other impacts and outcomes from society, could potentially lead to conflicting social responsibility practices among corporations, local communities and governments. Furthermore, the roles that society plays in social responsibility vary among countries, as each county has its own societal values and social norms. Consequently, the social domain requires deeper investigation of how society is shaping CSR and sustainability and its impact for change locally, regionally and globally. For example, sustainability "threatens the American dream" and "tramples on property rights and personal preferences" (O'Toole, 2013: p. 1). Another example is how the media often points blame at corporations that use philanthropy as public relations while simultaneously promoting unhealthy food to the public. The blame should not be pointed at corporations because many people in society do not always choose healthy food despite the health benefits of nutritious food. Thus, the freedom of personal preferences in social responsibility versus corporate and government social responsibility is not adequately addressed. Further to this, society requires corporations and government to take responsibility without reciprocation from society. Moreover, the freedom of personal preferences drives the social domain within culturally and socially constructed layers and has vast consequences for CSR and sustainability and other subject fields.

It is crucial that people cooperate for societal advancement and progress, but this is an ideal and not a fully shared endeavor by all stakeholders due to competing interests. Moreover, human and social relationships within the social domains of CSR and sustainability can be practiced based upon a social category to promote toleration, protection and avoidance of our differences and values for the sake of social responsibility. Furthermore, the defining concepts and categories found within the social domain could be implied as a formal and cultural way of sustaining socio-economic progress, national social control and social stability, and not social responsibility. Moreover, social responsibility could be a temporary solution that sustains short-term responsibility and long-term irresponsibility. Thus, the social domain in CSR and sustainability is a multidimensional construct that is in a constant state of flux and shifts purpose, functions and relationships within social systems and other systems. A potentially more accurate way of defining the social domain would be to include the factors and detriments that promote and sustain social fragmentation within "a variety of social responsibility domains" (Scruggs and Buren, 2014: p. 32).

Popular Social Domain Constructs in CSR and Sustainability

The social sciences as socio-economics have always played a role in the concept of CSR (Garriga and Melé, 2004). For example, consumer, employee and occupational health and safety are some of the socio-economic standards used to depict social responsibility in the social domain (Tumay, 2009). Consequently, an underdeveloped social domain drives CSR social initiatives within socio-economics. Mihelcic et al. define the social domain within sustainability as socio-economic driven: "the design of human and industrial systems to ensure that humankind's use of natural resources and cycles do not lead to diminished quality of life due either to losses in future economic opportunities or to adverse impacts on social conditions, human health and the environment" (2003: p. 5315). As a result, understanding economic and social processes within interactions among societal variables is inadequate (Meadowcroft, 1999). Furthermore, the human component of sustainability science may be following the social domains of CSR and sustainability in that the social is simply supporting the socio-economic needs and social benefits for society. Nevertheless, although some scholars in CSR and sustainability address decision-making and other psychological theories in understanding society within sustainability, the social impacts and outcomes are apportioned and portrayed as socio-economic progress and do not introduce greater social accountability and progress.

Carroll, a leading proponent of CSR, suggests the definition of social responsibility focuses on business responsibilities within economic, legal, ethical and discretionary demands from society as indicated in his Pyramid CSR model of economic, legal, ethical and philanthropic domains, and followed by his three overlapping economic, legal and ethical domains (Carroll, 1979, 1991; Schwartz and Carroll, 2003). However, these models do not explicitly suggest a social domain. It appears that the general definition of social is simply implied as individuals or organizations in society. Further to this, social responsibility is not required from society. Blindheim (2011) suggests attaining the common good in sustainability is contingent upon the legitimate operations and design of political institutions. However, Hayek (1960) argues there are many independent actors within the whole of society that need to be addressed by gradual and partial measures instead of the total amount. As a result, sustainability may constrain collective human behavior through social construction and prompt inquiry into whether sustainability is a collective outcome. Therefore, the common-good approach warrants examination of complex social processes, responses and attitudes.

The social domain simply supports the economic and environmental domains. Therefore, the social domain is simply a regurgitation of existing social categories and is not a factor in leading and fostering people into social responsibility. Thus, it is not the fault of disciplines. Rather it is the fault of society to expect social responsibility solely from institutions, thereby constructing societal expectations and social responsibility as self-serving.

Social Domain Constructs in Social Sustainability

Social sustainability captures many social categories such as the common good, socio-economics and societal well-being. The concept is generally defined as "to the degree of equality and social inclusion in a society where the gap between the richest and the poorest becomes too wide (especially if the riches are very narrowly concentrated in a few hands) society will degenerate into criminality, increasing social unrest and eventually into social revolution" (Stern et al., 2014: p. 30). As a result, the social in social sustainability is implicit and borrows from existing socio-economic categories. According to Magis and Shinn (2009), social sustainability achieved formal and international reputation following a 1987 report to the United Nations called World Commission on Environment and Development. The report noted that sustainable development requires focused attention on social, ecological and economic conditions in the world.

Social sustainability as defined by Agenda 21 consists of equity, empowerment, accessibility, participation, sharing cultural identity and institutional stability (Agenda 21, 2012; Khan, 1995). Nevertheless, emergent principles of social sustainability focus on human development and reinforce society's passive and fragmented participation, as meeting humanity's needs, welfare and well-being and not requiring from humanity consistent reciprocation and participation in the sustainability agenda. As a result, the growing interest in sustainability is challenging traditional disciplinary thinking in the social sciences (Redclift, 1999). The societal component of sustainability is generally defined as societal structures, institutions and social capital (Spangenberg, 1997). Further to this, Bossel's system determined basic orientators that include reproduction, psychological needs and responsibility that depict the human elements within the environmental basic orientators (2000). However, Littig and Grießier (2005) question societal change within social processes and structures to ensure the chances for development of future generations.

Social well-being (Prescott-Allen, 2001) and social development (Polanyi, 2001) play a central role in social sustainability. However, economic development and social development do not progress equally in sustainable development (Magis and Shinn, 2009). Furthermore, current meanings of CSR and sustainability are constructed within social categories that do not capture and result in equal accountability for all actors. Compounded with this challenge is the dilemma to ensure equal opportunities for all. Therefore, current social domain indicators do not adequately address specific social contexts for corporations and as a result provide questionable academic discourse and research for social sustainability (McKenzie, 2004) that can lead to constricting social performance in CSR and sustainability.

The Social Domain in Business

CSR and sustainable development are generally defined as three dimensions: economic, environment and social (Littig and Grießier, 2005). However, "very little literature has been published on how organizations can achieve success in all three areas at once" (Mersereau and Mottis, 2011: p. 33). It is clear from the literature that CSR and sustainability share common social definitions and goals. The social domain is ambiguously thrown about within the theories, models and methods of CSR and sustainability, omitting critical information about the role and impact of society from local communities, individuals, groups and so on in sustaining social responsibility. Despite the continual attempts of NGOs and various social movements in local communities to direct a lack of social responsibility towards corporations, it is rare to hear about the lack of social responsibility within local communities. Moreover, many people across sectors may agree with CSR and sustainability practices within the business culture and business strategies, while preferring individual and social freedom within a local community. This requires a paradigm shift in how people think, shape and potentially limit the development of the social domain within CSR and sustainability. New business models and social development indicators are needed. CSR cannot increase in legitimacy without society's reciprocation of social responsibility. Therefore, social controls within strategic, financial and governance factors are crucial for determining underlying social practices not captured and measured in corporate governance factors within CSR and sustainability (Filatotchev and Nakajima, 2014).

If people really want a better world and a better quality of life then examination of the social domain's role and impact in CSR and sustainability is warranted. As each country has differing and competing values, the pursuit of shared co-determination may lead to challenges in creating global, national, regional and local shared social values. Consequently, many companies are establishing a strategic social purpose for shared values (Shared Value Initiative, 2014) and creating social identities similar to branding identities (Graafland, Eijffinger and Smid, 2013). Moreover, "firms that are deeply embedded in their community often exhibit corporate social commitment and foster interactions with other field members" (Bansal, Gao and Qureshi, 2014: p. 953). Likewise, stakeholders have a say in the way products and services are delivered and are placed into the social domains of CSR and sustainability. Further to this, scholars are examining alternative organizations, such as employee ownership, social enterprises, creative cooperatives, community development, community land trusts, cutting-edge ownership, public pensions (Alperovitz, Dubb and Howard, 2007), and the social sector to create better ways of conducting business while creating value for society. Nevertheless, no matter how much society strives to renew business and economic development for the betterment and advancement of social progress, the strategic role of society apart from economic development must be evaluated. Therefore, why is it important to evaluate the social domain separate from economic development? Society and business do not reciprocate and share all societal values and norms within business and society. Consequently, some companies may look for opportunities to narrow the gaps of business and societal relations in business strategies, while other businesses may dismiss the challenges of sharing and examining differing business and societal relations, leading many companies to focus on strategies and initiatives within economic endeavors. Thus, evaluating the social domain within economic development does not provide a true picture of societal advancement and progress.

The Social Domain in Government

The government's role in CSR and sustainability plays an integral part in regulating and establishing legal forms, provisions, public policies and programs in partnerships with business and society and is a driver of CSR and sustainability (Moon, 2004; Aguilera et al., 2007; Barnett, 2007; Moon and Vogel, 2008; Thiel, 2010). CSR is a strong public-policy tool for governments within human, social and environmental development because it provides "social protections while strengthening national economic competitiveness" (Steurer, 2010: p. 1). Generally, the government is perceived to be self-enforced and voluntary within CSR and sustainability. However, the interplay between government and corporations can define government within CSR and sustainability as self-government, "facilitated by government, partnership with government, and mandatory by government" (Gond, Kang and Moon, 2011: p. 651). The social domain in CSR and sustainability consists of a broad range of social issues and is interpreted by many governments through a socio-economic democratic lens (Steurer, Margula and Martinuzzi, 2012) and has a plethora of pre-determined social categories such as human rights, education and so on, highlighting stakeholders' social and environmental concerns and interests within social caring and social responsibility (ibid.). Thompson, Teeuwen and Georgieva (2014) suggest a significant challenge to the social domain in government is a lack of political will to establish and enforce support for reshaping impacts and risks to human rights. A few CSR scholars depict the government playing a supportive role with the private sector at the helm to ensure that society activities within the "society-domain" are adequately accommodated (Othman and Abdellatif, 2011: pp. 286–7). Aslaender and Curbach (2015) propose "if corporations act as quasi-governmental actors and provide civic rights in communities, it remains unclear whether such engagement should be seen as a voluntary discretionary engagement, terminable at any time for any reason, or as an obligation resulting from corporate citizenry" (p. 3). Further to this lies the question of corporate capability and resources to effectively resolve societal problems in lieu of government engagement.

In addition, some governments enact national legislation requiring social and environmental reporting and through disclosure law (Shamir, 2010) and advance CSR initiatives within the forms of "awareness raising and capacity building" (Steurer, Margula and Martinuzzi, 2012: p. 12). Furthermore, the government plays a critical role in establishing regulations and social policies to foster social responsibility between corporations and local communities. As governments worldwide must determine how to invest in the future, corporations and local communities can play a key a strategic role to increase national, regional, and local competitiveness. For example, Gaines (2006) proposes that the social and economic spheres in sustainable development promote a broader national security framework. "Exploring security linkages in the sustainable development frame of reference thus opens our minds to broader, more complex, and ultimately more meaningful connections between personal security and the patterns of economic activity and social organization that affect human use and abuse of the environment" (Gaines, 2006: p. 324). However, challenges exist due to different groups in local communities and divided interests and beliefs that may be hidden within measures of national social control and social stability that could lead to increased national and personal security risk and decreasing national competitiveness.

Measuring the Social Domain

Many businesses are implementing social purposes and missions within the company's business model to improve social issues and social impacts (Social Impact Investment Taskforce, 2014a). Nevertheless, will data measurements sustain positive social impacts due to society's strategic role in sustaining social change and impact? What will be deemed as dependable social returns and social risk? Generally, measurement of the social domain is based upon socio-economic and well-being indicators and other various indices of the economic, social and environmental domains in CSR and sustainability (Giovanni, 2004). Proponents for an emerging market in social investments argue:

> Because impact measurement demonstrates an investor's true intent to have a positive impact, it is central to the practice of impact investing. Without it, effective impact investing cannot occur. Done right, impact measurement can:

> Generate intrinsic value for all stakeholders in the impact-investing ecosystem

> Mobilize greater capital to increase the amount of aggregate impact delivered by impact investing

> Increase transparency and accountability for delivering on intended impact. (Social Impact Investment Taskforce, 2014b: p. 3)

The financial indicators of the "impact value chain " are based upon socio-economic measures and not social measures (Social Impact Investment Taskforce, 2014b: p. 17). Measuring changes in society such as employment surrounding social issues is helpful, but these measurements do not address society's role and responsibility in sustaining social change and impact. This may not appear to be important or relevant to investors, who are primarily interested in financial returns, but without solid social domain indicators, processes and frameworks, the measurements will be simply measuring socio-economic impacts instead of social and societal impacts.

Assessing the impact of socially responsible investment, Campbell and Vick (2007) analyze UK legal disclosure requirements based upon voluntary CSR, financial market considerations, and national legislation.

> *People tend to distrust official (publicly) released information and resort to private means (such as bribery and word of mouth) to govern their transactions and interests. The government in a relation-based society tends to be less focused on social issues due to the lack of checks and balances in the political system, and citizens tend to have less say in social issues and less ability to influence social issues. In turn, firms face little public pressure to behave responsibly. Under such an institutional arrangement, firms feel neither obliged to communicate their social responsibility nor to act in the interest of the public. (Hu, 2014: p. 227)*

Investors, measurement and data service providers, regulators and policymakers, funders, researchers and standard setters should include the role and responsibilities of non-financial indicators within the social domain for mutual and ongoing accountability and learning of sustainable social impacts. Without society's reciprocation in social impact investing, the social value created will not be sustained because society is embedded into the social structures and social mechanisms of the social domain. For example, the Social Impact Investment Taskforce has identified emerging trends that include market convergence, financial quantification and unforeseen external impacts that will form future impact measurement (2014b). Social impacts from individuals, groups and local communities should be included in these measurements because accountability from investors without accountability from society can limit social responsibility.

Broadening the study of social impacts beyond socio-economics to include the determinants and detriments within the human and social processes in the internal and external unforeseen impacts are a more accountable and solid objective for sustainable social impacts. This would better determine social development, social progress and social stability instead of measuring, increasing and decreasing social impacts. An example of social internal determinants and detriments that lead to an external social impact is Reihlen and Ringberg's definition of a socio-cognitive approach. Managers may be

> *forced to reframe existing cultural models to make sense of a situation and thereby create a unique mental model. This is referred to as a 'private model.' Some private models continue to remain private, whereas others become shared and 'objectified' through the interaction and negotiation with other managers, thereby entering into the broader social fabric of a company and the wider community. (Reihlen and Ringberg, 2013: p. 17)*

Reconstructing the Social Domain

Individual construction of CSR and sustainability has created multiple realities and differing theories and practices. However, despite the differing constructed views, the social domain remains to be the least developed and least important domain within CSR and sustainability. Perhaps, it is society's constructed view of social responsibility as required in business and not in the local community. Social construction of objective reality is a mixed filter portraying subjective reality as objective truth (Gallimore, Goldenberg and Weisner, 1993). Likewise, CSR and sustainability reporting is socially constructed to determine sense-making for optimal measurements to improve social responsibility within economic, social and environmental dimensions. Further to this, collaboration among multiple stakeholders remains incorporeal (Melhus and Patton, 2013). Perhaps each domain's methodology is simply "a labeling device for social control" (Gergen, 1985: p. 268) and "offers no truth through method" (ibid., p. 272) resulting in social responsibility as pretense. Thus, less distinction of social discipline boundaries is required to decrease pretense in social responsibility for improving meaning and sense-making of social responsibility among corporations, local communities and governments (Gergen and Gergen, 2008). Moreover, "responsibility does not arise from within people nor can it be imposed externally by some supraindividual body. Rather, it depends on the structure and form of our social relations and the way people are located within them" (McNamee and Gergen, 1999: p. 79). Furthermore, the local community's role is oftentimes "culturally constructed" for its own collective future (Gergen and Gergen, 2000: p. 4).

Society's Role in the Social Domain

Who holds society accountable? Why is this important? Human society "will affect the shape of future market behavior" (Pawel, 2009: p. 34). Likewise, non-market actors can influence and shape the behavior and function of market actors due to vicarious learning, symbols, forethought, self-reflection, self-efficacy and self-regulation (Pajares, 2002). Furthermore, it is people who determine what is valuable, and promote and sustain how the social domain should be defined as "any social system is changing all the time" (Dowd, 2014). Consequently, heterogeneous nations broadly control for diversity and inclusion. Therefore, the social domain should be examined separately because people compete by differing shared societal values and expectations that could lead to unstable and limited prosperity in societies and in business.

Conscious capitalism is an example of how changes are primarily focused to change capitalism's impact on society but not require change from society (Mackey and Sisodia, 2014). Likewise, the Creating Shared Value Initiative (Porter and Kramer, 2011), the Organization for Economic Co-operation and Development's Measurement for Economic and Social Progress (OECD, 2013) and the Social Progress Index 2013 and 2014 are simply creating socio-economic value for society. Individuals who "receive their basic human needs, foundations of wellbeing, and opportunities for reaching full potential" (Porter, Stern and Artavia Loria, 2013: p. 53) are inadequate to drive social progress but adequate to drive socio-economic progress. Furthermore, just as "a narrow conception of capitalism" (Porter and Kramer, 2011: p. 2) has led to business not realizing its potential to support societal challenges and needs, a narrow concept and understanding of the society's role in the social domain in CSR and sustainability has led to corporations and government not addressing and examining the potential of all stakeholders to sustain social responsibility, national competitiveness, and social advancement and progress.

The Social Domain

This volume unveils the social domain in CSR and sustainability by developing greater understanding of social responsibility within local communities, corporations and governments; identifying and reducing unequal social responsibility outcomes from local communities, governments and corporations; and identifying a weak and inadequate social domain in CSR and sustainability. Moreover, it will help local communities, corporations and governments to identify and manage challenges and gaps in social responsibility in CSR and sustainability and establish greater understanding of the role of society through examination of multiple realities of social responsibility among local communities, governments and corporations and the impacts for local, regional and national competitiveness. Overall, it will provide practical tools for business, government and local community leaders faced with challenging societal constraints and consumer and public demands on a daily basis from differing cultures, sectors and industries. Readers of this volume will be in a better position to manage and develop CSR and sustainability strategies in a volatile global economy by bridging differing industry and sector partnerships among local communities, governments and business worldwide, which is so crucial for successful managers and leaders in companies, local communities and governments.

CHAPTER 1

The Interchange of Societal Values and Beliefs, Trust, Competitiveness and Expectations within CSR and Sustainability

This chapter will discuss four social responsibility knowledge gaps in CSR and sustainability and three drivers of CSR and sustainability that provide a foundation of how society co-creates, changes expectations and drives social responsibility among local communities, corporations and governments worldwide. In addition, a brief overview of the qualitative and quantitative research methodology with a discussion of societal values/beliefs, trust, competitiveness and expectations will be examined within CSR and sustainability.

Changing Societal Expectations in Social Responsibility

Social responsibility within business is a complex circumstance and is not focused solely on increasing profits and enhancing reputation management. "Self-image concerns" may drive how individuals and groups promote social responsibility (Benabou and Tirole, 2010: p. 3). On the other hand, "when everyone behaves in a socially responsible way, no one gets credit for it" (ibid., p. 7). Thus, changing societal expectations require corporations to critically evaluate social trends and social responsibility in a "competitive world" (Uddin, Hassan and Tarique, 2008: p. 2000). Where do societal expectations originate and how do they fuse to become accepted by the corporation? It can be argued it is due to unregulated CSR reporting (Mersereau and Mottis, 2011). Society is socially constructing global social responsibility rules and frameworks for communicating corporations' social responsibly such as the International Labor

Organization (ILO), UN Global Compact, Global Reporting Initiative (GRI), Dow Jones Sustainability Index (DJSI), Socially Responsible Investing (SRI), Integrated Reporting (IR) and so on. These frameworks seek to institutionalize CSR on a global level through the creation of norms, rules and standardized procedures for CSR thereby creating "isomorphic pressure to institutionalize CSR in business" (Brammer, Jackson and Matten, 2012). Accordingly, if society expects corporations and governments to go beyond compliance then society must follow. Is social responsibility just another formal legal process whereby non-criminal forms of responsibility are socially acceptable in society? Bernabou and Tirole (2010) suggest economic agents may want to promote values that are not shared by lawmakers. Furthermore, "human sociality" highlights the tendencies of individuals to seek social status, to build and maintain social identities, and to cooperate with others under certain conditions (World Bank Development Report, 2015: p. 42). Since social preferences are heterogeneous, it is inevitable that some consumers, investors or workers' values will not be fully reflected in policy. Clearly, social responsibility encompasses values that must be changed. Values have always played a primary role in shaping society (Wartick and Wood, 1998). Societal norms and values play an integral role in business success. However, corporations have the same citizenship expectations as society (Freeman, 2002). Therefore, it can be argued, business values are simply a reflection of society's values. Further to this, Porter and Kramer's "shared value" strategic approach reveals how companies try to meet local communities' expectations (2006: p. 1). There is further logic in that culture distinguishes corporations from each other (Schein, 1985) just as local community cultures select their preferred culture. Consequently, corporations and local communities have heterogeneous values and preferences that may be shared and diffused. Likewise, "society's values and current levels of knowledge are reflected in companies' activities and companies are judged according to current standards" (Van Marrewijk and Were, 2003; Noren, 2004). However, Kumar and Kumar propose the "non-existence of markets for many biological resources imply that the social value of biological resources can't be derived from simple aggregation of their values to individuals in society, the sum of their private values" (2007: p. 812). Therefore, value judgments are necessary to determine uncertainties, risk and lack of knowledge (Weterings and Opschoor, 1994). In contrast, Swanson's (1995) research findings on corporations' value-driven (Maignan and Ralston, 2002) CSR initiatives are not dependent upon external social pressures. Further to this, should corporations integrate society's values or should corporations limit society's values and demands as these values may reduce a firm's capacity to progress and compete?

Rights and freedoms play a critical role in social responsibility and are not static and universal. Moreover, rights and freedoms may consist of varying societal standards that are complex, socially driven outcomes and expectations of societies and communities who maintain and select their preferred or local expectations within the household or local community, while demanding universal expectations from businesses. As a result, specific social constraints should be managed to increase corporate profits. Moreover, "social and environmental performances are not seen as an end in themselves but as a source of competitive advantage or a condition to be competitive" (Valor, 2005: p. 199). Therefore, it can be argued, reciprocal societal standards must be managed and carefully selected by corporations resulting in the implementation and growth of business CSR activities as associated with erosion and dismantling of institutionalized social solidarity (Kinderman, 2010). It is clear from the social responsibility literature that people carry their individual values and beliefs with them regardless of established social norms or laws resulting in a deeper and multilayered social domain among local communities, corporations and governments. Social responsibility overlaps societal progress and societal advancement to increase individuals and local communities' capacity for national and global competitive advantage within economic, environmental and social means above and beyond socio-economic progress. Moreover, the study investigated possible associations and outcome expectancies of the variables between local communities, governments and corporations.

Four Knowledge Gaps in Social Responsibility in the Social Domain

There is much literature published about the role of CSR and sustainability for corporations and governments (Clarkson, 1995; Williams and Aguilera, 2008). However, little attention is paid to the one-sided social domain concepts of sustainability and CSR (Wiersum, 1995; Littig and Grießier, 2005; Marquis, Glynn and Davis, 2007) as corporations carry the weight of social responsibility while government initiates regulatory behavior for societal welfare leading to a lack of reciprocal social responsibility and sporadic participation from local communities. In addition, the social domain is discussed significantly less than the environmental and economic domains (Opp and Saunders, 2013). In general, scholars depict social responsibility in CSR as business and society reciprocation (Bowen, 1953; Heald, 1970; Preston and Post, 1975; Wood, 1991; Carroll, 1999; Margolis and Walsh, 2001; Orlitzky, Schmidt and Rynes,

2003; Dentchev, 2004; Garriga and Melé, 2004; Kotler and Lee, 2005; Falck and Heblich, 2007). The Iron Law of Social Responsibility indicates that "society grants legitimacy and power to business. In the long run, those who do not use power in a manner which society considers responsible will lose" (Davis, 1973: p. 314). Moreover, according to Carroll (1979) it is the role of business leaders to decide which domains of CSR the company will emphasize and implement. Thus, the company is responsible for the impact of its decisions and activities on society and the environment including the health and welfare of society, expectations of stakeholders, and compliance with laws consistent with international norms of behavior. This further displays "social responsibility being accountable for the social affects the company has on people—even indirectly" (Uddin, Hassan and Tarique, 2008: p. 205). Evidently, social responsibility has developed with businesses managing societal responsibility expectations, leaving social responsibility the obligation of corporations instead of society, and resulting in four knowledge gaps.

KNOWLEDGE GAP ONE: SOCIO-ECONOMICS AS SOCIAL RESPONSIBILITY

Consumer, employee and occupational health and safety are some of the socio-economic standards used to depict social responsibility in the social domain (Tumay, 2009). Consequently, an under-developed social domain drives social responsibility within socio-economics. As a result, understanding economic and social responsibility within interactions among societal variables is inadequate (Meadowcroft, 1999). Furthermore, the human component of sustainability science may be following the social domains of CSR and sustainability in that the social is simply supporting the socio-economic needs of society. Although some scholars use decision-making and other psychological theories to understand society and social responsibility within sustainability, the social impacts and outcomes are apportioned and portrayed as socio-economic progress and do not introduce greater social responsibility.

KNOWLEDGE GAP TWO: SOCIAL WELL-BEING AND
SOCIAL DEVELOPMENT AS SOCIAL RESPONSIBILITY

Social well-being (Prescott-Allen, 2001) and social development (Polanyi, 2001) play central roles in social sustainability. However, economic and social development does not emerge and move in balance within sustainable development (Magis and Shinn, 2009). Therefore, highlighting the primary role of societal well-being creates limitations to the advancement of the social domain of sustainability. Furthermore, the emphasis on societal welfare and social well-being appeases the social domain as supporting people's needs and issues while promoting a passive and sporadic participatory role of society in sustainability. Moreover, focusing on societal well-being issues such as gender equality, equity, participation and social justice is supporting social fragmentation due to differing individual and societal ontological preferences.

Parris and Kates (2003) describe the social domain in sustainable development as a community of cultures, groups and places, society institutions, social capital, states and regions and people concerned with child survival, life expectancy, education, equity and equal opportunity while Dahlsrud identifies the social domain of CSR as "the relationship between business and society" whereby corporations "contribute to a better society," "integrate social concerns in their business operations" and "consider the full scope of their impact on communities" (2006: p. 4). Thus, individuals are autonomous and free to create value for themselves in line with the mutual interests of stakeholders without reciprocation from the corporation. Furthermore, companies seem to have the upper hand in how poverty reduction will proceed through "profit-making, win-win situations and consensus outcomes in multi-stakeholder arrangements" without critical "developing impact assessment" (Prieto-Carron et al., 2006: p. 978). As an illustration, the local community provides permission for a company to develop operations and receive benefits from the company's financial and social contributions to the local community (Freeman, 2002).

KNOWLEDGE GAP THREE: SOCIAL RESPONSIBILITY OF STAKEHOLDERS

Examining stakeholder engagement is vital for understanding societal expectations and social responsibility within the social domain of CSR and sustainability (Freeman, 1984; Freeman, Harrison and Wicks, 2007). Similarly, sustainability challenges are complex problems that necessitate stakeholder participation (Wiek et al., 2012a). Alon et al. (2010) portray stakeholder concerns within the community as culture, education, well-being, public safety, and protection of the natural environment. Nevertheless, there are differing levels of engagement that could change at any time and impinge on a corporation's sustainability initiatives negatively. Therefore, focusing on key stakeholders helps to provide better management of societal uncertainty and complexity. However, some CSR scholars suggest measurement inaccuracies

(Waddock and Graves, 1997) and potential future events (Ulmann, 1985) that promote theoretical and empirical restrictions of the social domain. Furthermore, "current sustainability science efforts do not sufficiently engage with the affected and responsible stakeholder groups, and fail in contributing significantly to solution options and transformational change" (Wiek et al., 2012b). This may result in stakeholder unsuitability (Wood and Jones, 1995) and limitations of relationships between corporations and society. For instance, "roles of CSR in community development refer to the ways the responsible behavior is perceived by a community of stakeholders and how impacts are felt by them" (Ismail, 2009: p. 207). This implies corporations are responsible for societal benefits without reciprocation from society. As a result, corporations are limited in their social impacts and initiatives because society separates itself from the responsibility relationship and deliberates responsibility to the corporation.

KNOWLEDGE GAP FOUR: UNEQUAL SOCIAL RESPONSIBILITY AMONG CORPORATIONS, LOCAL COMMUNITIES AND GOVERNMENTS

Developing a society based on meeting its needs without responsibility and competitiveness is unsuitable. Furthermore, not all uncertainties within the social decision-making domain will be resolved (Newig, Pahl-Wostl and Sigel, 2005). Corporations frequently struggle with local community engagement and responsibility. Nolan, Shipman and Rui describe perplexing situations in which local norms and local human rights may be contradictory (2004). Sustainability indicators should be stratified to include local indictors within local communities (Corbiere-Nicollier et al., 2002) and develop over time as communities become involved and existing conditions change (Carruthers and Tinning, 2003). Moreover, the social domain in CSR and sustainability does not adequately address society's role in social responsibility. Instead, the social domain describes people surrounding CSR and sustainability initiative and issues. Furthermore, the social domain is defined as romanticizing innocent people in society with rights and privilege of sporadic participation that demand higher social responsibility standards from governments and corporations without reciprocation to the governments or corporations upon whom they depend for their well-being.

CSR and sustainability definitions, theories and methods are socially constructed in similar and very diverse ways, and are crucial for understanding multiple realities of social responsibility within local communities, governments and corporations. Furthermore, the social domain has many differing definitions, methods and theories of society's role and the local community's role in social responsibility resulting in non-reciprocal and unequal social responsibility from local communities to corporations. Consequently, a more accurate representation of social responsibility could be accomplished through investigating society's role and construction of CSR and sustainability with corporations and governments. Moreover, where do CSR and government responsibility end and the local community's responsibility begin? "Responsibility, does not arise from within people nor can it be imposed externally by some supraindividual body. Rather, it depends on the structure and form of our social relations and the way people are located within them" (McNamee and Gergen, 1999: p. 79). In addition, the local community's role is oftentimes "culturally constructed" for its own collective future (Gergen and Gergen, 2000: p. 4). Apparently, personal and societal freedom precludes responsibility from the informal society requiring the formal society within institutions and partnerships and alliances to sustain social responsibility while individuals and local communities within the informal society are free to drive and construct social responsibility ad hoc. Henceforth, the social domain is socially constructed and sustained by the formal and informal society due to unequal social responsibility among local communities, governments and corporations.

Overview of Qualitative and Quantitative Methodology

In order to understand how corporations, governments and local communities impact each other, an examination of practitioners' values and beliefs, trust and competitiveness in CSR and sustainability is necessary. Evaluating the social domain in CSR and sustainability requires qualitative methods to describe perceptions of social responsibility instead of quantifying social cause and effect for the generation of new knowledge (Pini, 2004). The methodology incorporates a global multilevel micro–meso–macro framework to challenge current primary constructs of the social domain. The micro system domain is defined as individual and the macro system domain will be defined as social. The meso dimension will focus on a variety of differing micro and macro changing dynamics within the independent and dependent variables. This framework will help to determine gaps in social and individual construction of social responsibility among corporations, governments and local communities. Since the social domain consists of complex phenomenon, a mixed-mode design utilizing positivist and interpretive methods within a quantitative and qualitative research framework was implemented to examine possible relationships of differing and multiple realities of social variables (Burns and Grove, 2005).

The data results provide guidance on how practitioners from corporations, governments and non-profit organizations and NGOs perceive trust, competitiveness and values and beliefs and how these shape, direct and impact relationships and social responsibility challenges among local communities, governments and corporations. The survey and interview questions defined CSR and sustainability as economically driven with environmental and social aspects. The social aspects acknowledge wealth alone does not promote and sustain the well-being and success of a society. Furthermore, social responsibility contains components of societal progress and societal advancement to increase individuals and local communities' capacity for national and global competitive advantage within economic, environmental and social means above and beyond socio-economic progress.

Thematic analysis was utilized for practitioners' answers to interview questions. A web-based survey collected data from practitioners worldwide. SPSS version 20 was used for descriptive and inferential statistics of the web survey variables. Primary theories selected are integrative, instrumental, political and ethical theories (Garriga and Melé, 2004). Complementary theories are risk perception, cultural, evolutionary, group selection bias, competitiveness theory and realist theory of emergence.

The practitioners' gender, age groups, management levels, educational levels, sectors, industries and locations from the web-based survey interview questions responses include private, public (federal, state, local) nonprofit/ NGO across industries such as agriculture, chemical, office supplies, industrial, food and beverage, natural environment, consumer goods, services and information technology located in North America, Switzerland, Romania, India, Japan, Netherlands, the United Kingdom, Vietnam, France, Spain, Ghana, Afghanistan, Germany and Africa. Data from the web-based survey interview questions were collected from staff (non-management), management and senior management in corporations, federal, state and local governments, non-profits/NGOs worldwide within individuals, groups, organizations, country, regional, local, ethnicity, gender and educational levels.

The research methodology design examines the economic, environmental and social domains of CSR and sustainability with a particular focus on how the practitioners construct the "social" in the social domain to determine social responsibility among governments, corporations and local communities.

Consequently, the hypotheses and research questions examine social responsibility among corporations, governments and local communities within the lack of reciprocal social responsibility and sporadic participation from individuals and local communities and its potential impact on local, regional and national competitiveness.

Independent variables such as age, management level, education, ethnicity, and gender were used to ensure high levels of internal external validity for the sample population size. For identification description of potential relationships in social responsibility, dependent variables such as social responsibility, values and beliefs, trust and competitiveness, along with significant themes, major patterns and numerical analysis were employed to examine possible relationships, patterns and themes between the dependent and independent variables in the quantitative and qualitative data. The dependent variables are interdependent and were interpreted and measured based upon descriptive, thematic analysis and inferential analyses. Competitiveness measures how people perceive high performance impacts in collaboration and in individual initiatives. Social responsibility is measured as a task and decision-making variable based upon laws, regulations, policies and differing cultural interpretations, expectations and social construction. Trust measures perceptions and judgments of how people trust others that are known and not known across society levels. Lastly, values and beliefs are measured as opinions and judgments of how people think, behave and construct social responsibility in CSR and sustainability in partnerships and day-to-day activities.

Local communities are defined as local citizens, local governments and non-profit organizations due to the government and corporations' direct involvement in the local community. Determining how to measure the social processes collectively at the local community level is a challenge. Social cohesion is constrained within differing and changing values and it is misleading to believe that social cohesion can be sustained primarily through economic growth. Moreover, social cohesion within local communities may promote conflict and contribute to a divided and fragmented city (Forrest and Kearns, 2001). Furthermore, competitiveness theory is a demanding task due to the complex and varied factors of competitive processes (Snieska and Bruneckiene, 2009).

Some reporting errors are always evident in social science research studies due to human subjectivity and situational and instrument mechanical factors. Encouraging honest responses are a challenge due to expected social norms and organizational values. Participants were not required to provide their actual age. Therefore, it is not possible to determine if there are any overlapping ages with the age groups. Social desirability was also considered as a potential limitation in participant responses. Other limitations include the participants' interest in the research topic and questions as opposed to other populations. Another possible bias is the frequency in which the participants take web-based surveys and participate in discussions on CSR and sustainability thereby resulting in findings that do not represent the general population within the countries' national, regional and local populations.

Three hypotheses investigated how social responsibility determines the social inputs and outputs among local communities, governments and corporations and their impacts for local, regional and national competitiveness. The hypotheses are:

- If local communities are held accountable for social responsibility by corporations then local, national and regional competitive advantage will increase.
- If governments hold local communities accountable for national competitiveness and social responsibility then local communities will become a driving force for national global competitive advantage.
- If local communities hold governments, and corporations accountable for social responsibility then local, national and regional competitive advantage will increase.

Linear regression was administered to test the independent (age, gender, education, management level and ethnicity) and dependent variables (social responsibility, competitiveness, values, beliefs and trust) to determine the strongest relationship in explaining practitioners' attitudes towards social responsibility and the social domain in CSR and sustainability among local communities, governments and corporations.

PRACTITIONERS' VALUES AND BELIEFS OF CSR SUSTAINABILITY

Most practitioners from various countries describe sustainability as sustainable development similar to the Brundtland Report with three pillars that emphasize the environmental pillar over the economic and social pillars. Examples from the survey text include, "use the Brundtland definition," "meeting today's needs without compromising the future," "preserve our resources" and "sustainable development with three pillars" (see Appendix).

Practitioners from the USA include social responsibility as an implicit characteristic of sustainability. Harmony defines sustainability in Japan, evolution is critical in Spain while France adds creating shared values with a strong emphasis on corporate driven sustainably initiatives. Generally, sustainability is described homogenously across management levels as a three-pillar continual process in sustainable development: "three pillars," "three pillar holistic," "three pillar equity," "the process of continued use" and "three pillar long-term." Sustainability across age groups is generally defined as sustainable development with three pillars consisting of economic, environment and social domains with a strong focus on the environmental dimension. However, the 30–45 age group include creating shared values as corporate driven initiatives. Both genders describe sustainability as economic, social and environmental pillars with an emphasis on the environment. Practitioners across educational levels generally describe sustainability as economic, social and environmental pillars with an emphasis on the environmental domain: "environment driven," "environment politically driven term," "environmental stewardship," "preservation profit" and "environment preservation." The participants' responses were stratified as White, Black, Hispanic and Asian ethnic categories in the USA, Europe, Africa and Asia locations with specific countries as described by the participants in their text responses. They all describe sustainability as sustainable development with three pillars consisting of economic, environment and social domains and highlight, "three domain long-term survival," three pillar long-term," "Brundtland definition," "three pillar prosperity" and "three pillar equity." Europeans highlight "three pillar business strategy" and "three pillar balance." In particular, the Spanish focus on "evolution without destruction."

Some practitioners across countries view CSR and sustainability interchangeably: "business imperative," "local, regional and global platforms," "all three required for long-term global population," "the company developed a natural solution in a sustainable way" "transforming the lives of human beings and existing systems." CSR in Japan "requires an ethic for everything," thereby limiting individual freedom. France is focused on "balance prosperity," while "public policy" drives CSR in India. CSR requires a "sustainable lifestyle" in Romania. The USA defines CSR as the "right efforts and terms," whereas Afghanistan emphasizes "relationships and "serving others." Most practitioners in all countries define social as "interactions with others," "me vs. others vs. me," "investigative journalism" and "human rights." In contrast, CSR portrays greater heterogeneity with some practitioners at management and non-management levels uncertain of the meaning of social responsibility: "CSR is separate from sustainability," "requires ethics for everything," "wrong terms," "I do not know what it is" and "dedicated leadership."

A practitioner in senior management believes companies can implement CSR separately from sustainability. Likewise, a practitioner in management suggests moving from a focus on social responsibility to a sustainability focus. Other practitioners describe corporations as lacking genuine concern for social responsibility. For example, a practitioner from management comments: "Companies appear to be acting more socially responsible until the media unearths information about their bad practices—like bribing other countries to get out around regulations. Makes it difficult to have a lot of faith in what companies preach (e.g., Walmart)."

Another practitioner in management states: "Only a few take up any social responsibility." A senior management participant argues: "Corporations never want to be socially responsible. But the public policies of different countries make them or rather hold them responsible." Likewise, a practitioner in non-management comments: "True CSR exists in rare instances where the corporate leadership is truly committed/morally compelled, otherwise, there is much green washing corporate bring about. It is the individual responsibility of shareholders and consumers to hold large corporations accountable."

On the other hand, a practitioner in management provides insight into companies that demonstrate social responsibility in the organizations' business strategy and states,

> *The company I work for has a purpose to develop natural solutions in a sustainable way, green chemistry for animal husbandry crop rising. It is today essential to produce food in quantities to feed 9 billion people in 2050 but this has to be done in the respect of animals and nature. The range we develop is made for welfare, hygiene efficiency of animal nutrition, using less antibiotics chemicals such as pesticide. Working for this company, I have the feeling to work in a sustainable spirit. It was part of the reason I wanted to work for it.*

CSR is represented with greater heterogeneity than sustainability across age levels. A practitioner within the 18–29 age group suggests communicating CSR to people who do not know about CSR in local communities (Table 1.1): "But there has to be someone to transfer these messages to the local people who have not heard about corporate social responsibility." Most practitioners describe CSR as uncertainty of correct terms and definitional constraints. CSR is defined as corporate driven across educational levels with some uncertainty from practitioners in the doctorate, graduate and undergraduate levels: "drives business," is "corporate driven" and produces "prosperity" and "uncertainty." CSR across ethnic groups resulted in heterogeneous comments within ethnic categories: "corporations never want to be responsible," "few are responsible," commercial word limitation," "radical transformation," "local knowledge," "limits sustainability," "social is limited to people—not all three," and "balance of progress over time."

TABLE 1.1   VALUES AND BELIEFS OF SUSTAINABILITY AND CSR: PRACTITIONER QUOTES
BY AGE GROUP

Age group	Sustainability	CSR
18–29	"sustainable development"	"CSR is important for modern day business"
30–44	"Brundtland definition long-term" "environment management system"	"creating shared values" "corporate leadership driven"
45–60	"3 legged long-term" "production, preservation and profit" "environment driven"	"commercial wording" "for the greatest good for the longest time"
60–75	"3 pillars long-term" "environment driven"	"accountability is critical to creating a truly equitable and balanced society"

In general, practitioners' comments across age groups highlight CSR as corporate trust fragmentation and corporate driven initiatives. Practitioners across management levels generally define social in CSR as social welfare, community and external interactions with others. Competitiveness in CSR included comments from management such as increasing accountability, social welfare and is individually and relationally driven. A practitioner in management argues: "competitiveness is not to be put against social responsibility, but with it."

The social in CSR is defined homogenously across age groups resulting in external interactions with others. Some differences within age groups include a focus on social welfare, human rights and the common good. Further definitions of the social domain in CSR include external interactions with others, societal well-being and welfare within the doctorate, graduate, and undergraduate levels with an individual focus from practitioners with some college education. Overall, social was defined as external interactions with others across ethnic groups: "involvement of people in society," "interacting with others," "orientations interactions with others" and "relationships between people."

Three Drivers of CSR and Sustainability

DRIVER ONE: COMPETITIVENESS

Competitiveness in CSR and sustainability is a strategic approach of many companies (Collins and Porras, 1996; Makower, 1994; Scott and Rothman, 1992; Dutta, Lach and Rustichini, 1995; Gladwin, Kennelly and Krause, 1995; Reinhardt, 1998; Hoppe and Lehman-Grube, 2001) for first-mover advantage and to enhance improvement (McWilliams and Siegel, 2000). Other companies may also include resource strategies for environmental social responsibility (Hart, 1995; McWilliams, Van Fleet and Cory, 2002). Since competitive advantage is defined as an economics driven phenomenon in CSR, this is the primary reason competitiveness is not defined within a social context of CSR and sustainability. It is observable that human evolution and culturally adaptive systems are competing and strategically played in human-environment systems. Human-environment systems play a strategic role in resilience to natural and human activity disturbances (Mayer, 2007). Therefore, competing human and social systems should be reflected in CSR and sustainability to evaluate human and social impacts on environmental systems, and unevenly proportioned social responsibility among local communities, governments and corporations.

Competitiveness in CSR is also driven by relationships (Carroll and Shabana, 2010) and is an integral part of the widening and deepening of market-relations and of the re-structuring of social relations away from post-war institutions (Kinderman, 2011). Relationships can drive new norms that articulate the social expectations for business (Scott, 2004). However, the lack of recognition of societal responsibility and social competitiveness values in the societal progress indexes (Bečić, Mulej and Švarc, 2012) promote little social and personal development in local communities that is so crucial for determining social responsibility among local communities, governments and corporations. For example: Are competitors stakeholders? Is the local community a competitor?

Business and societal competitiveness is vital for social progress. However, CSR and sustainability currently establish competitiveness as the sole responsibility of corporations for economic development. Since competitiveness is relationally driven in CSR and sustainability, how can corporations sustain social responsibility without reciprocation from local communities? Furthermore, how can corporations remain competitive in social responsibility if the local community does not reciprocate? As a consequence, competitiveness in CSR and sustainability is economics and not socially driven because local communities do not reciprocate social competitiveness, thereby leaving corporations to compete economically.

TABLE 1.2 COMPETITIVENESS BY DEMOGRAPHIC FACTORS

Demographic factor	CSR, CSP, and sustainability are dependent upon competetiveness		I believe it is the responsibility of community members to increase national competetiveness and social responsibility	
	Mean	SD	Mean	SD
Gender				
male	3.94	0.84	4.06	0.80
female	3.94	0.84	4.06	0.80
Total	3.88	0.89	4.15	0.81
Age				
18–29	3.94	0.97	4.53	0.62
30–45	3.76	0.97	4.04	0.74
45–60	3.88	0.82	4.04	0.82
60–75	4.17	0.75	4.33	0.82
Management lovol				
non-management	4.11	0.68	4.17	0.62
management	3.82	0.95	4.20	0.88
senior management	3.83	1.03	3.92	0.79
Education				
some college	3.67	1.16	4.67	0.58
undergraduate degree	4.25	0.46	3.88	0.84
graduate degree	3.82	0.98	4.13	0.76
doctorate degree	3.92	0.83	4.21	0.88
Location				
Africa	4.50*	0.71	4.50	0.71
Asia	3.86	1.03	4.36	0.75
Europe	3.37	1.07	4.11	0.66
USA	4.03	0.62	4.09	0.82
Ethnicity				
Asian	3.87	0.99	4.33	0.72
Black	4.00	1.00	4.33	0.58
Hispanic	4.00	1.00	3.67	1.16
White	3.82	0.87	4.10	0.76

Note: Items scored 1 (definitely false) – 5 (definitely true); N = 81. *$p < 0.10$ ANOVA test for difference in mean scores across demographic factor.

The second section of the survey focuses on competitiveness within CSR, corporate social performance (CSP), sustainability and social responsibility. Table 1.2 presents descriptive statistics of two survey items that addressed competitiveness. There was no significant difference in the mean competitiveness score across gender, age, management level, education or ethnicity. However, mean scores for "CSR, CSP, and sustainability are dependent upon competitiveness" were significantly different across nationalities, with the highest endorsement occurring in Africa, followed by the USA. Additionally, overall item endorsement by practitioners was higher for the item, "I believe it is the responsibility of community members to increase national competitiveness and social responsibility."

In general, most practitioners define competitiveness as an economics driven feature in CSR and sustainability that is individually and relationally driven, with added comments on values and beliefs regarding the importance of relationships with others (see Appendix). Competitiveness is generally described across age groups as contextually driven by accountability, government, corporations, stakeholders, management, culture, values and beliefs and within age groups highlighting ethics and relational levels. Both genders define social responsibility in CSR and sustainability as a competitive and economic driven feature that is socially constructed: "a responsible society is competitive," "limits freedom," "societal good," "culturally contextual," "societal benefits," "sustainability is social responsibility," "future balance prosperity," "business driven," "economic driven," "economic growth" and "corporate driven."

Competitiveness across ethnic groups was heterogeneous with the exception of practitioners in Hispanic, Asian and White categories: "various sense of values," CSR and CSP determine competitiveness," "not related to CSR," "global standards limitation," "collaborative competition," "high performance," "government policy driven" and "growth limitation." The Hispanic, Asian and White practitioners' commented that the concept of competitiveness has a definitional limitation: "word definition limitation," "we should do better, not necessarily more" and "growing faster than the world is not the way."

DRIVER TWO: TRUST

Table 1.3 presents the distinction between personal and relational trust. Table 1.4 presents the distinction between particular and general trust.

"General trust is based upon universal propensity to trust others" (Luo, 2005: p. 438), and particular trust "exists only in particular dyads" (ibid., p. 439). The distinction between general trust and particular trust was inferred from participant responses on survey items that assessed self-reported trust for various general and particular targets. For example, "trust of the neighborhood" and "trust of the government" are considered general trust, whereas "trust of family" is considered particular trust. As shown in Table 1.4 mean trust for particular targets was higher than mean trust for general targets (e.g., "trust of family" mean = 2.86, "trust of neighborhood" mean = 2.15).

Likewise, trust is generally understood as trust earned over time," "contextual" or simply portraying a lower level of trust in people and generally such as "people would probably take advantage of you" (see Appendix). Trust is defined within the parameters of general and particular trust. However, a practitioner in the 45–60 age group comments, "too old to trust everybody and everything" implying that trust may decrease in age. Comments of trust from males resulted in particular and general trust, while females focused on particular trust. One female practitioner commented: "There is a gender issue missing here—I have had many coworkers, local businesses and others take advantage of women—therefore I have lost trust."

Practitioners within the doctorate and graduate levels describe trust as particular and general, while the undergraduate and some college education levels focus on particular trust. Practitioners across educational levels highlight values and beliefs as ethics and relational levels. Competitiveness is defined heterogeneously across educational levels. The Hispanics Asians, and Whites describe trust as particular: "internal relationship driven," "I trust in my family and God. All the rest is relative." "Do I know them personally or not?" "trust is not easy to give right from the beginning," "trust is earned over time" and "trusting completely makes it difficult to choose." General trust was highlighted among Romanians and Afghans: "In each and every step of life trust is important to keep relationships and develop our business." "A positive construction responsible in continuing the good things. We solidarize to recreate on a solid foundation of our society."

TABLE 1.3   PERSONAL AND RELATIONAL TRUST BY DEMOGRAPHIC FACTOR

Demographic factor	Personal trust is essential to sustainability, CSR and CSP		Sustainability, CSR and CSP are dependent upon relational trust		I work aggressively to develop trust with my local community	
	Mean	SD	Mean	SD	Mean	SD
Gender						
male	4.57*	0.91	4.24	0.82	3.44	0.98
female	4.06	1.03	4.23	0.67	3.58	1.06
Total	4.36	0.99	4.23	0.76	3.50	1.01
Age						
18–29	4.06	1.18	4.12	1.05	3.47	1.07
30–45	4.24	0.97	4.04	0.74	3.54	1.02
45–60	4.60	0.82	4.32	0.69	3.44	1.00
60–75	4.50	1.23	4.50	0.55	3.50	1.05
Management level						
non-management	4.00	1.09	4.06	0.54	3.00*	1.09
management	4.47	0.96	4.37	0.73	3.69	0.87
senior management	4.64	0.81	3.92	1.17	3.67	1.07
Education						
some college	4.67	0.58	4.67	0.58	4.50	0.71
undergraduate degree	4.25	1.04	4.25	0.46	3.50	1.31
graduate degree	4.34	0.94	4.18	0.76	3.49	1.02
doctorate degree	4.37	1.14	4.17	0.96	3.42	0.88
Location						
Africa	5.00	0.00	4.50	0.71	2.00	1.41
Asia	4.00	1.23	3.71	1.20	3.64	0.75
Europe	4.16	1.02	4.32	0.67	3.33	1.24
USA	4.56	0.82	4.26	0.62	3.59	0.96
Ethnicity						
Asian	4.07	1.21	3.73	1.16	3.60	0.74
Black	5.00	0.00	4.33	0.58	2.33	1.16
Hispanic	4.00	1.41	4.00	1.41	2.50	2.12
White	4.36	0.96	4.30	0.61	3.55	1.02

Note: Items scored 1 (definitely false) – 5 (definitely true); N = 81. *$p < 0.05$ ANOVA test for difference in mean scores across demographic factors.

TABLE 1.4 TRUST FOR VARIOUS GENERAL AND PARTICULAR TARGETS BY DEMOGRAPHIC FACTOR

Demographic factor	Trust family		Trust church		Trust neighborhood		Trust government		Trust corporation		Trust people you meet	
	Mean	SD	Mean	SD	Mean	SD	Mean	SD	Mean	SD	Mean	SD
Gender												
male	2.85	0.36	1.92	0.69	2.07	0.46	1.86	0.47	1.86	0.57	1.85	0.36
female	2.87	0.34	2.04	0.69	2.25	0.57	1.84	0.45	1.75	0.62	1.97	0.40
Total	2.86	0.35	1.97	0.69	2.15	0.52	1.85	0.46	1.81	0.59	1.90	0.38
Age												
18–29	2.88	0.33	1.60**	0.63	2.29	0.47	1.88	0.60	2.06	0.43	1.94	0.25
30–45	2.92	0.28	1.79	0.63	2.12	0.67	1.84	0.47	1.76	0.72	1.88	0.53
45–60	2.80	0.41	2.21	0.59	2.08	0.39	1.81	0.40	1.69	0.55	1.92	0.27
60–75	2.83	0.41	2.50	0.84	2.17	0.41	1.83	0.41	1.83	0.41	1.83	0.41
Management level												
non-management	2.72	0.46	1.82	0.73	2.06**	0.42	1.72**	0.58	1.72	0.58	1.83	0.38
management	2.88	0.32	1.92	0.60	2.27	0.50	2.00	0.31	1.91	0.52	1.95	0.38
senior management	3.00	0.00	2.25	0.87	1.75	0.45	1.42	0.52	1.50	0.62	1.83	0.39
Education												
some college	3.00	0.00	2.50	0.71	2.33	0.58	1.67	0.58	2.00	1.00	2.00*	0.00
undergraduate degree	2.88	0.35	2.00	0.54	1.88	0.35	1.75	0.46	1.88	0.64	1.75	0.46
graduate degree	2.87	0.34	1.90	0.75	2.22	0.48	1.87	0.40	1.73	0.55	2.03	0.28
doctorate degree	2.83	0.38	1.96	0.69	2.08	0.58	1.83	0.57	1.92	0.58	1.75	0.44
Location												
Africa	2.50	0.71	1.50*	0.71	1.50	0.71	1.00*	0.00	2.50	0.71	1.50	0.71
Asia	2.93	0.27	1.57	0.65	2.00	0.39	1.86	0.66	2.00	0.56	1.93	0.27
Europe	2.89	0.32	1.83	0.72	2.37	0.60	1.68	0.48	1.89	0.57	2.06	0.42
USA	2.88	0.33	2.19	0.64	2.14	0.49	1.97	0.30	1.63	0.60	1.91	0.28
Ethnicity												
Asian	2.87*	0.35	1.60	0.63	2.00	0.38	1.87	0.64	2.00*	0.54	1.93	0.26
Black	2.33	0.58	1.67	0.58	1.67	0.58	1.33	0.58	2.33	0.58	1.67	0.58
Hispanic	2.67	0.58	2.00	1.41	2.00	0.00	1.33	0.58	1.00	0.00	2.00	0.00
White	2.92	0.28	2.12	0.68	2.24	0.56	1.88	0.39	1.76	0.59	1.94	0.38

Notes: Items scored 1 (do not trust) – 3 (trust completely); N=81. *$p<0.05$ ANOVA test for difference in mean scores across demographic factor. **$p<0.01$ ANOVA test for difference in mean scores across demographic factor.

DRIVER THREE: VALUES AND BELIEFS

Social responsibility encompasses values that must be changed. Similarly, societal construction of knowledge and norms are reciprocated among corporations, governments and local communities according to current societal standards in social responsibility. Furthermore, society and individuals create value based upon their own preferences that may lead to decreasing local, regional, national and global competitive advantage. Should corporations incorporate society's values or should corporations restrict societies' values and concerns as these values may reduce a firm's capacity to progress and compete? Nolan, Shipman and Rui (2004) suggest that "companies must be responsible for implementation and respect of rights and freedoms" and should not be held responsible for "all international rights and freedoms because the states do not uphold basic rights." Dynamic social systems are driven by societal expectations that differ based upon situational context. For instance, rights and freedoms in local communities and the household do not share the same universal societal standard in companies. For these reasons, companies should evaluate conflicting narrow and holistic societal impacts within the economic, social and environmental domains in CSR and sustainability.

Therefore, reciprocal societal standards require cautious selection by corporations for growth of business CSR activities as associated with erosion and dismantling of institutionalized social solidarity (Kinderman, 2010). Thus, meeting society's expectations without societal reciprocation weakens a company's capacity to foster and sustain social responsibility.

The final section of the web survey evaluated practitioners' self-reported values and beliefs about such targets as the environment, money, work, local community, relational trust and community competitiveness. The descriptive statistics of several survey items that addressed "values and beliefs" are presented in Tables 1.5 and 1.6.

Values and beliefs are depicted as socially driven and constructed for females and males: "good working relationships," "require relations with others," and "continuously cultivate the relational levels of life" (see Appendix). Values and beliefs were described as question limitations from the Spanish and Americans: "God said to work make money by wealding—only delinquents work without effort including speculators," "hard work, luck and connections are linked and not separate." Asian and European practitioners depicted values and beliefs as ethics: "good working ethics, relationships," "ethical values" and relational levels. Some Europeans highlight, "relational levels of life" and "serve others in the community."

TABLE 1.5   ATTITUDE TO ENVIRONMENTAL PROTECTION BY DEMOGRAPHIC FACTOR

Demographic factor	Protecting the environment should be given priority, even if it causes slower economic growth and some loss of jobs		Protecting economic growth and creating jobs should be given priority, even if it reduces environmental protection	
	n	%	n	%
Gender				
male	21	30.9	17	25.0
female	17	25.0	13	19.1
Age				
18–29	10	14.7	4	5.9
30–45	13	19.1	12	17.6
45–60	11	16.2	12	17.6
60–75	4	5.9	2	2.9
Management level				
non managoment	7	10.1	9	13.0
management	25	36.2	16	23.2
senior management	7	10.1	5	7.2
Education				
some college	1	1.4	2	2.9
undergraduate degree	2	2.9	6	8.7
graduate degree	24	34.8	13	18.8
doctorate degree	12	17.4	9	13.0
Location				
Africa	1	1.6	1	1.6
Asia	8	12.5	5	7.8
Europe	6	9.4	11	17.2
USA	21	32.8	11	17.2
Ethnicity				
Asian	8	12.3	1	9.2
Black	1	1.5	1	3.1
Hispanic	2	3.1	2	1.5
White	25	38.5	26	30.8

Note: N=81.

TABLE 1.6 VALUES AND BELIEFS BY DEMOGRAPHIC FACTOR

Demographic factor	Money		Work		Local community		Relational trust		Individual competetiveness		Community competetiveness	
	Mean	SD	Mean	SD	Mean	SD	Mean	SD	Mean	SD	Mean	SD
Gender												
male	3.88	0.50	4.17	0.62	3.74	0.83	4.17	0.85	3.98*	0.81	3.60	0.83
female	3.83	0.65	4.17	0.65	3.63	0.72	4.38	0.68	3.45	0.99	3.27	0.79
Total	3.86	0.56	4.17	0.63	3.69	0.78	4.25	0.79	3.76	0.92	3.46	0.82
Age												
18–29	3.88	0.33	4.06	0.56	3.41	0.94	4.00	0.87	3.71	1.11	3.59	0.87
30–45	4.00	0.60	4.26	0.69	3.91	0.67	4.35	0.65	3.87	0.97	3.43	0.84
45–60	3.73	0.45	4.15	0.46	3.65	0.75	4.36	0.57	3.84	0.69	3.50	0.71
60–75	3.67	1.03	4.00	1.10	3.67	0.82	4.00	1.55	3.17	0.98	2.83	0.98
Management level												
non-management	3.89	0.47	4.00	0.69	3.44	0.98	4.22	0.88	3.22**	0.94	3.00**	1.14
management	3.86	0.57	4.19	0.63	3.79	0.57	4.22	0.82	4.02	0.72	3.69	0.56
senior management	3.92	0.67	4.25	0.45	3.92	0.67	4.33	0.49	3.92	0.79	3.33	0.78
Education												
some college	3.67	0.58	4.67	0.58	4.00	0.00	3.67	0.58	4.00	1.00	3.67	0.58
undergraduate degree	3.75	0.46	3.88	0.84	3.75	0.71	4.50	0.54	3.88	0.99	3.75	1.04
graduate degree	3.76	0.59	4.11	0.61	3.61	0.89	4.32	0.88	3.68	1.00	3.42	0.76
doctorate degree	4.08	0.50	4.29	0.55	3.75	0.68	4.13	0.68	3.83	0.76	3.37	0.88
Location												
Africa	4.00	0.00	4.50	0.71	3.00*	1.41	5.00	0.00	5.00	0.00	5.00*	0.00
Asia	4.07	0.48	4.21	0.58	4.00	0.78	3.93	0.83	4.14	0.95	3.64	0.93
Europe	3.82	0.64	4.18	0.53	3.29	0.85	4.35	0.61	3.59	0.94	3.29	0.69
USA	3.71	0.52	4.06	0.68	3.77	0.69	4.26	0.83	3.68	0.84	3.43	0.70
Ethnicity												
Asian	4.07	0.46	4.20	0.56	4.00	0.76	3.93	0.80	4.13	0.92	3.60*	0.91
Black	4.00	0.00	4.33	0.58	3.33	1.16	4.67	0.58	4.67	0.58	4.67	0.58
Hispanic	3.33	0.58	4.33	0.58	4.00	0.00	3.50	0.71	4.00	1.41	3.33	1.16
White	3.79	0.58	4.10	0.66	3.56	0.80	4.35	0.76	3.58	0.90	3.33	0.75

Note: Items scored 1 (not important) – 5 (extremely important); N=81. *p<0.05 ANOVA test for difference in mean scores across demographic factor.
**p<0.01 ANOVA test for difference in mean scores across demographic factor.

Social Responsibility Implications

Current social domain constructs in CSR and sustainability contribute towards unbalanced social responsibility among corporations, governments and local communities. The literature of CSR and sustainability drive social responsibility within a narrow social domain portraying the social as socio-economic, social sustainability, social welfare, social well-being and stakeholders. Consequently, the narrow social domain often limits social responsibility among corporations, governments and local communities. The lack of social responsibility from local communities sustains questionable societal values and expectations and decreases social progress due to a lack of critical social and personal development that is crucial for increasing social responsibility among local communities, governments and corporations. Furthermore, competitiveness in CSR and sustainability is relationally driven, thereby requiring greater societal competitiveness and social responsibility from local communities for reciprocation to corporations and governments. Therefore, an under-developed social domain and unequal social responsibility reveals gaps in the knowledge of CSR and sustainability resulting in unequal and fragmented social responsibility among corporations, governments and local communities.

CHAPTER 2

Six Constituents of Social Domain Fragmentation in CSR and Sustainability

This chapter reviews the ways in which the social domain is depicted and fragmented in CSR and sustainability deriving from current theories, methodologies and definitions resulting in six constituents that drive social domain fragmentation in CSR and sustainability. Generally, CSR and sustainability are discussed as two disconnected concepts or as interchangeable and separate. This chapter begins with a broad discussion of CSR and sustainability definitions, various social domain theories and methodologies followed with analysis of the challenges and limitations of social responsibility within current sustainability and CSR frameworks. A comprehensive discussion of how the social domain's focus on socio-economics, societal well-being, social sustainability and stakeholders is considered to limit society's role in social responsibility. Finally, the chapter closes with an examination of social responsibility constructs such as societal values and expectations, social progress and business and societal competitiveness in CSR and sustainability and how these constructs are linked to social responsibility in the social domain and its implications among corporations, governments and local communities.

Evolution and Definitions of CSR

It is important to highlight similar and varying definitions and methodologies of CSR and sustainability as this will create a foundation for the examination of the social domain in CSR and sustainability. There is no known specific originating date for CSR. De Bakker, Groenewegen, and Den Hond (2005) suggest little unanimity concerning the actual evolution of CSR. Generally, the responsibility concepts of CSR emerged out of the progressive era with Adam

Smith (Wartick and Cochran, 1985) and the Quakers in the seventeenth and eighteenth centuries (Amaeshi et al., 2007). Spector (2008) suggests the origins of CSR began between 1945 and 1960 when CSR aligned capitalism against communism. Other scholars suggest CSR originated in 1953 with Bowen's Social Responsibilities of Businessmen (Wartick and Cochran, 1985; Gond and Crane, 2008). Carroll, a leading proponent of CSR, defined and moved social responsibility to corporate social responsibilities (Windsor, 2001; Garriga and Melé, 2004; Gond and Matten, 2007) developing a pyramid framework of CSR that is widely recognized and used by proponents of CSR (Windsor, 2001). Each dimension of CSR is still highly contested terrain—how much corporations should set the agenda, what standards for social responsibility are acceptable and to whom the company is ultimately responsible (Brammer, Jackson and Matten, 2012). Furthermore, CSR is frequently defined broadly with no consensus (Votaw and Prakash, 1973; Banerjee, 2001). Overall, the concepts of CSR developed within different theories and approaches such as shareholder value, strategic competitive advantage, marketing, corporate constitutionalism, integrative social contract theory, corporate citizenship, issues management, public responsibility, stakeholder management, corporate social performance, stakeholder normative theory, universal rights, sustainable development and the common good (Garriga and Mele, 2004; McWilliams, Siegel and Wright, 2006).

CSR THEORIES AND METHODOLOGIES

CSR literature lacks consensus for a standard definition. Typically, many people who are familiar with the concept will initially define CSR within the three domains of the social, economic and natural environments. In general, CSR literature covers a vast array of theories and methods resulting from a multitude of terms, which are continually being replaced by new terms in business and society. Moreover, sustainability is often implemented to depict good intentions and outcomes (Karoly, 2013) and continues to develop differing terms with little convergence (Ratiu and Anderson, 2014). However, some scholars suggest five common distinctions of CSR as "voluntariness, responsibility, creation of value, plural objectives, and respect for man and nature" (De Prins et al., 2009) or overlapping relative rules (Matten and Crane, 2005). Aguilera et al. define CSR as "beyond the narrow economic, technical and legal requirements of the firm to accomplish social (and environmental) benefits along with the traditional economic gains which the firm seeks" (2007: p. 836). Unsurprisingly, CSR has also been described as corporate citizenship and corporate social performance (McWilliams, Siegel and Wright, 2006).

Furthering the complexity of broad CSR definitions and methodologies is how each theory and method addresses the social domain of CSR. Gond and Matten suggest that "the current limitations of the field lie in its limited conceptual appreciation of CSR as a social—rather than just a corporate phenomenon," which contributes towards "a narrow understanding of CSR as a social phenomenon" (2007: p. 3) which explains most of the challenges encountered in theory building and assessment (Aguilera et al., 2007). Furthermore, broad differences in CSR may account for explicit organizational responsibility in societal interests and implicit norms, values and rules responsibility within formal and informal institutions (Matten and Moon, 2008). Overall, most social and broad CSR methodologies inspire companies to engage with their stakeholders voluntarily in their business practices (Shamir, 2005) resulting in limited social performance. Graafland, Eijffinger and Smid (2004) summarize methodological concerns among CSR ethicists such as monism, commensurability of various values, disregard of intentions, subjectivity of valuation, context versus moral actions, problems of communication, stakeholder inequality and company control that intimately result in social performance fuzziness. Furthermore, CSR methodologies are inconsistent (Waddock and Graves, 1997; Margolis and Walsh, 2001; Ruf et al., 2001; Van Beurden and Gossling, 2008). Some CSR social methodologies highlight philanthropy and key stakeholders (Longo, Muran and Bonoli, 2005; Sasse and Trahan, 2007) while other CSR methods employ legal compliance (Juholin, 2004) combining a variety of CSR variations (Quazi and O'Brien, 2000; Uhlaner, Van Goor-Balk and Masurel, 2004). Overall, most social and broad CSR methodologies encourage companies to interact with their stakeholders voluntarily in their business practices (Shamir, 2005). It is clear that social and broad CSR methodology and theories are varied originating from a diffused and corporate construct resulting in limited social performance.

The Mirror of CSR and Sustainability

Before examining the definitions and methodologies of sustainability, it is beneficial to briefly emphasize how CSR and sustainability sometimes mirror each other, as this will provide a broad social domain scope for discussion of social responsibility within the social domain. Examination of philosophy, such as in Aristotle and Kant, and other subject fields within the natural environment suggest the concepts of CSR and sustainability has been around for many decades. As a consequence, CSR may simply be a social construction (Kumar and Kumar, 2007; Dahlsrud, 2008). Likewise, sustainability is primarily normative and socially constructed (Haughton, 1999; Lafferty and Meadowcroft, 2000; Huge and Waas, 2011). Nolen, Shipman and Rui (2004) suggest that CSR is the way in which businesses create sustainable development. Similarly, Huge and Waas (2011) suggest, CSR is interpreted in his own way and incorporates sustainable development as its motherhood concept.

Sustainability Properties and Assessments

Similar to CSR, there are a plethora of sustainability definitions and methods (Lopez, Garcia and Rodriguez, 2007; Huge and Waas, 2011). Sustainability literature is often partitioned into environmental domain, environmental and social domains, or ecological, economic and social domains (Wiersum, 1995; Littig and Greßier, 2005). Parris and Kates (2003) suggest sustainability differs globally due to differing metrics and varying definitions, data and methodologies. Moreover, Costanza and Patten (1995) suggest most definitions of sustainability infer current actions will create durability in the future thereby creating a sustainable life system. As a result, sustainability has frequently been described as a 'wicked' problem (Norton, 2005; Brundiers and Wiek, 2010; Raffaelle, Robinson and Selinger, 2010). Furthermore, the concept of sustainable development is defined abstractly (Batie, 1989; Lele 1991; Norgaard, 1994).

The Narrow Social Domain of CSR and Sustainability

As previously discussed, the social domain in CSR and sustainability is an outcome of varying CSR and sustainability definitions and methodologies. Therefore, an analysis of primary constituents of social dimension constructs and methods such as societal well-being, socio-economics, social sustainability and stakeholders that are used to describe the social domain in CSR and sustainability is warranted. This analysis will help determine the limitations and challenges of social responsibility frameworks among local communities, governments, and corporations.

CONSTITUENT ONE: THE SOCIAL DOMAIN AS SOCIO-ECONOMICS

The social sciences as socio-economics play a primary construct in CSR (Garriga and Melé, 2004) and are often described as consumer, labor and occupational health and safety (Tumay, 2009). However, that role is very limited and has not developed within the social domain of CSR, as most CSR social initiatives are not intended to tackle social issues beyond socio-economics. The social dimension of CSR and sustainability is difficult to define and primarily focuses on economic and environment dimensions with a focus on the socio-economic benefits and welfare of society. On the other hand, Amaeshi, Osuji and Nnodim suggest there is "widespread agreement on some form of corporate responsibility for social issues" (2008: p. 3).

Mihelcic et al. define the social within sustainability as socio-economically driven to ensure "that humankind's use of natural resources and cycles do not lead to diminished quality of life due either to losses in future economic opportunities or to adverse impacts on social conditions, human health and the environment" (2003: p. 5315). Likewise, Turner et al. (2003) define the human conditions as social and human capital and endowments (population, entitlements, institutions, economic structures), which can be summarized as socio-economic conditions. Moreover, neo-classical economics determines how people respond to the cost of gains and losses in environmental inquiry (Daly, 1977; Jacobs, 1991; Ekins, 1992; Norgaard, 1994; Redclift, 1999). The human component of sustainability science may be following the social domains of CSR and sustainability in that the social is simply meeting the socio-economic needs of society. Furthermore, sustainable development is primarily driven by economic and environmental factors and does not equally embed the social domain as a key factor in successful development. Although some scholars use decision-making and other psychological theories to understand society within sustainability, the social impacts and outcomes are measured and depicted as socio-economic progress and do not incorporate more of social progress. For example, environmental planning generally defines the social dimensions as socio-economic systems and social learning (Selman, 1999).

Clearly, socio-economics plays a strong role in social performance of CSR and sustainability. However, the focus on socio-economic growth is inadequate for social responsibility. Corporations are reporting their social activities, but it is difficult to determine social progress and social performance due to an under-developed social domain. Consequently, the economic domain drives sustainability followed by environmental and social aspects in sustainable development.

CONSTITUENT TWO:
THE SOCIAL DOMAIN AS SOCIAL WELFARE AND WELL-BEING

Societal welfare and well-being appear to be another way of establishing the social domain in CSR and sustainability. For example, Prieto-Carron et al. focus on poverty reduction in developing countries of the global South and suggest "that a critical research agenda needs to be concerned with the creation of new ways of systematically assessing the impact of CSR social issues such as poverty, wages and workers' and conditions in general" (2006: p. 983). Noren (2004) suggests that corporations improve societal welfare and well-being through protection of their workforce. Likewise, "businesses are to effectively promote social welfare due to the fact that they exist as a response to a social need and have a privileged financial position in the society" (Iamandi, 2007: p. 7). However, varying dimensions of social life reveal progression and regression within societal plans that may not result in positive advancement (Meadowcroft, 1999).

Are differing inequalities among stakeholders justified if they raise the level of the poor (Freeman, 2002)? Clearly, on the one hand, individuals and groups create value that is not reciprocated to the corporation. On the other hand, corporations must manage win–win situations among a wide range of stakeholders for sustainable development benefits between local communities and corporations. As a result, society's role in the social domain shapes and directs the role of local communities and governments in social responsibility while limiting the role of corporations in social responsibility.

CONSTITUENT THREE: STAKEHOLDERS AS THE SOCIAL DOMAIN

Stakeholders are an obvious component of a corporation's success and are a primary method of CSR (Freeman, 1984; Alkhafaji, 1989; Anderson, 1989; Meznar, Chrisman and Carroll, 1990; Preston and Sapienza, 1990; Brenner and Cochran, 1991; Brummer, 1991; Clarkson, 1991; Goodpaster, 1991; Wood, 1991; Hill and Jones, 1992; Hosseini and Brenner, 1992; Prahalad and Hamel, 1994). Moreover, CSR is often driven by the stakeholders (Carroll, 1979; Wood and Jones, 1995; Carroll 1999). This suggests stakeholder power is vital for participation and decision-making in corporate determination (Arnstein, 1969; Burchell and Cook, 2006; Jonker and Nijhof, 2006; Burchell and Cook, 2008). Generally, stakeholders can be defined as "any group or individual who can affect or is affected by the achievement of the organization's objectives" (Freeman, 1984: p. 46).

How stakeholders should be considered and categorized is questionable (Lépineux, 2003). Apparently, society is described as stakeholders (De Bakker, Groenewegen and Den Hond, 2005). Dahlsrud (2008) reviewed definitions of CSR and found stakeholder and social dimensions received the same frequency counts in Google searches. The stakeholder model by Freeman broadly defines stakeholders as owners, suppliers, management, employees, local community and customers. In contrast, Noren describes stakeholders as "trade unions, owners, shareholders, investors, bankers, auditors, insurance companies, consumers, staff, financial analysts, suppliers, customers, competitors, future employees, media, NGOs, national authorities, local authorities, neighbors, surrounding environment (environment, public health and safety, sustainable development) and politicians" (2004: p. 8). However, Clarkson (1995) classifies stakeholders as suppliers, customers, employees, shareholders and community and suggests corporations must deal with stakeholders and not society.

Stakeholder dialogue should be fostered by authentic motives, trust and fairness (Phillips, 1997; Swift, 2001). However, "stakeholder mismatching" (Wood and Jones, 1995: p. 229) suggests limitations of relationships between corporations and society. Some CSR scholars suggest that the stakeholder theory consists of descriptive (no-moral-value statements) and normative (moral-value statements) aims (Donaldson and Preston, 1995; Garriga and Melé, 2004; Loranzo, 2005; Ulrich, 2008). For example, in community development, corporations are delegated social responsibility from society for meeting societal well-being criteria, resulting in social responsibility gaps between local communities and corporations. Consequently, this limits social responsibility development and growth between local communities and corporations.

In summary, improving methods of social responsibility research and measurement are warranted to better understand society's role and impact in developing and sustaining social responsibility standards among corporations, local communities and governments. Moreover, social data are qualitative data. Thus, it is easier to use socio-economic, societal welfare and well-being data as distinct conclusive quantitative evidence of social impacts, performance and responsibility.

CONSTITUENT FOUR:
UNEQUAL SOCIAL RESPONSIBILITY IN THE SOCIAL DOMAIN

Socio-economics, societal well-being and welfare, and stakeholders overlap and work together to form the primary constructs in the social domain, which result in unequal social responsibility. Dynamic social systems are driven by societal expectations that differ based upon situational context. For instance, rights and freedoms in local communities and the household do not share the same universal societal standard in companies. For these reasons, companies should evaluate conflicting narrow and holistic societal impacts within the economic, social and environmental domains in CSR and sustainability.

Overall, social responsibility has evolved with business managing society's social responsibility expectations, leaving social responsibility, the obligation of corporations and not society.

CONSTITUENT FIVE: SOCIAL PROGRESS IN THE SOCIAL DOMAIN

Sustainable development has a long history debating the qualities of social progress. Seager, Sellinger and Wiek argue that "while the advances of science and technology during the last 40 years have been extraordinary, it is not clear that they have contributed significantly to resolving complex problems of social progress" (2011: p. 469). Similarly, CSR is defined as how an organization integrates social, environmental and economic concerns into their values, culture, decision making, strategy and operations in a transparent and accountable manner and thereby establishes better practices within the firm, creates wealth and improves society (Benabou and Tirole, 2010). Thus, it is difficult to determine if CSR and sustainability contributes to societal progress due to human intentions and decision-making. Huge and Waas argue that sustainability "ultimately depends on societal and political will" (2011: p. 647). Meeting society's expectations without societal and political will to improve society weakens a company's capacity to foster and sustain social responsibility.

Social learning is frequently discussed in the sustainability literature. According to Selman, social learning is part of an "active citizenship and participatory democracy" where "opinions and skills are developed during the process of engagement" (1999: p. 174). How much should companies take responsibility when local communities can learn and participate at will? "The apparently self-evident statement that companies should accept responsibility is, in reality, not so simple" (Noren, 2004: p. 15). Furthermore, income and poverty driven social responsibility limits crucial reciprocation from local communities for effective social responsibility with corporations and governments. Therefore, why is society demanding social responsibility from corporations and not from local communities? Are local communities more socially responsible than corporations? Does society support one standard of social responsibility and progress for individuals and another standard for corporations? (Windsor, 2001). Why does there appear to be differing social learning in local communities and corporations? It could be argued this is due to the greater wealth creation opportunities of businesses and local communities justification and demands for greater social responsibility from corporations than from themselves. If society is not willing to contribute to solve societal problems, then government will lack the revenue to do its job and will require corporations to drive social responsibility (Avi-Yonah, 2006). Clearly, this approach depicts society as having strong control over corporations with little or no reciprocation from society to corporations. Moreover, it suggests corporations cannot demand strong social responsibility from society, but society can demand much social responsibility from business. Furthermore, it could be argued that local communities may have greater impact on social progress than corporations due to the less selective demands and views of social progress in local communities. Further to this, is social responsibility the job of corporations rather than government? (Levitt, 1958; Friedman, 1970). It is obvious that social progress is a vital component of social responsibility because it challenges and addresses the lack of social responsibility and social competitiveness in society beyond legal compliance within the social domain of CSR and sustainability.

CONSTITUENT SIX:
BUSINESS AND SOCIETAL COMPETITIVENESS IN THE SOCIAL DOMAIN

CSR is viewed as a driver of competitive advantage (Donaldson and Preston, 1995), corporate reputation (Porter and Kramer, 2006; McWilliams, Siegel and Wright, 2006; Branco and Rodrigues, 2006) and sustainable competitive advantage (King, 2002; Adams and Zutshi, 2004). As a result, governments are viewing CSR codes of conduct as a cost-effective means to enhance sustainable development strategies and as a component of their national competitiveness strategies to compete and position their exports globally (Petkoski and Twose, 2003). In contrast, some scholars such as Marcus and Anderson (2006) find various factors that influence CSR and competitive advantage. For example, progressive corporations and financial institutions view CSR and sustainable investments as a competitive advantage or a minimum requirement for risk mitigation (Petkoski and Twose, 2003). Likewise, managing community relations may reduce risk thereby creating an opportunity for competitive advantage (Berman et al., 1999).

Many scholars propose that competitive advantage in CSR is strongly influenced by the economic domain. As a result, there is little attention paid to how the social domain can play an equally important role in competitive advantage. Competitive dynamics and interactions among corporations, local communities and governments provide a foundation to examine unequal and competing social responsibilities that overlap and impact the domains in CSR and sustainability. Moreover, CSR can help consumers to identify with a particular brand (Bhattacharya and Sen, 2003) thereby enhancing the "transactional and relational outcomes in a real-world, competitive context" (Du, Bhattacarya and Sen, 2007: p. 225). Relational motives can drive new norms that articulate the social expectations for business (Scott, 2004). Moreover, relational motives within a company's industry group may often depress a company's instrumental motives (Aguilera et al., 2007). Likewise, Bansal and Roth (2000) suggest that companies may be significantly motivated by relationships followed by instrumental motives with moral motives as least significant. However, the role of societal competitiveness clearly leads to social progress, thereby requiring stronger social and individual development in local communities to better understand how competitiveness and social responsibility is shaped and practiced among corporations, local communities and governments.

Currently, the theory and practice of CSR and sustainability are driven largely by the voluntary nature of stakeholders without accountability from the government, civil and business sectors. Apparently, local communities are not held to the same social responsibility standards as corporations. Rather, it is corporations and governments. Corporations and governments can be self-serving, but so can society. Furthermore, local communities form their own united groups or corporations. Therefore, why is this issue not being addressed in theories of CSR and sustainability? Why should local communities be trusted for economic and societal progress without accountability from corporations and governments? Stakeholder accountability is necessary due to how local communities create meaning and power to express and maintain their self-interest, reliability and competitive advantage over other groups. Furthermore, without responsible and competitive stakeholders, sustainability and CSR will not produce sustainable value locally, nationally, regionally or globally.

How can corporations sustain social responsibility without reciprocation from local communities? Likewise, how can corporations remain competitive in social responsibility if the local community does not reciprocate? It can be argued that competitiveness in CSR and sustainability is economics and not socially driven because local communities do not reciprocate social competitiveness, thereby leaving corporations to compete economically. Thus, changing individual and social preferences are critical for valuation and require a deeper understanding of individual preferences and decision-making because a competing strategic culture in organizations and local communities sustains itself by efficacy capacity.

Social Domain Implications

CSR and sustainability are complex social phenomenon that focus on social responsibility within corporations and governments and are driven and measured by local community and stakeholder interests and corporate management (Clarkson, 1995; Matten, Crane and Chapple, 2003; Johnson and Onwuguegbuzie, 2004; Newell, 2005; Pater and Van Lierop, 2006; Cooper and Owen, 2007; Godfrey and Hatch, 2007; Gond and Matten, 2007; Marquis, Glynn and Davis, 2007; Gond and Crane, 2008; Owen, 2008). As a result, there is much information about the role of CSR and sustainability for corporations and governments (Clarkson, 1995; Williams and Aguilera, 2008). In addition, environmental and economic dimensions are addressed greater than the social dimension (Opp and Saunders, 2013). However, there are neglected and one-sided social domain concepts of sustainability and CSR (Wiersum, 1995; Littig and Grießier, 2005; Marquis, Glynn and Davis, 2007). For example, corporations carry social responsibility while governments develop and implement regulations for public welfare with voluntary social responsibility and participation from local communities. Therefore, an under-developed social domain and unequal social responsibility portrays CSR and sustainability as individual, societal and organizational reputation management.

Current social domain constructs in CSR and sustainability limit and contribute towards unequal social responsibility among corporations, governments and local communities. CSR and sustainability drive social responsibility within a narrow social domain portraying the social as socio-economic, social sustainability, social welfare, social well-being and stakeholders. Consequently, the narrow social domain creates unequal social responsibility among corporations, governments and local communities and decreases the acknowledgement of social progress that is crucial for increasing social responsibility among local communities, governments and corporations. Lastly, CSR and sustainability demonstrate that competitiveness in CSR and sustainability is relationally driven, thereby requiring greater societal competitiveness and social responsibility from local communities for reciprocation to corporations and governments.

CSR and sustainability are driven primarily by society, resulting in socially constructed institutions that are implemented according to economic needs and not social issues or concerns. Furthermore, the social is often depicted as socio-economic due to the lack of CSR and sustainability methods to effectively measure complex social processes. There are positive and negative outcomes of social construction. For example, society requires business social responsibility without reciprocation from local communities. Furthermore, the current meanings of CSR and sustainability are constructed within social relationships that do not result in equal social responsibility for all actors. Consequently, social responsibility may result in pretense.

CHAPTER 3

Human Bias and Social Responsibility Fragmentation in CSR and Sustainability

This chapter will discuss human bias and fragmentation in social responsibility derived from competing cultural, discipline and knowledge preferences among local communities, governments and corporations. Further discussion will include seven CSR and sustainability fragmentation challenges, stratification of human and social bias fragmentation and bias and social fragmentation challenges in key global CSR and sustainability reporting tools.

Human Bias and Social Responsibility Fragmentation

Laws do not change human bias. Rather, laws permit people to select personal modes of thinking that remain hidden and managed in public. For example, formal or external partnerships are sustained by the purpose and mission of the partnership, while informal or internal partnerships often embrace people who share similar values and beliefs. People strive to make the external outcomes such as a formal partnership equal for all, yet it is the internal processes that sustain a human and social bias.

Table 3.1 shows the practitioners' knowledge of sustainability, stratified by gender, age, management level, education, location and ethnicity. As shown, 58 practitioners reported knowledge about sustainability (72%), 47 reported knowledge of CSR (58%), and 27 reported knowledge of corporate social performance (33%). Since most practitioners reported that they were unfamiliar with CSP in the survey and the interviews, this chapter and Chapter 5 focus predominantly on CSR and sustainability.

TABLE 3.1 FREQUENCY DISTRIBUTION OF PRACTITIONERS' KNOWLEDGE ABOUT SUSTAINABILITY STRATIFIED BY GENDER, AGE, MANAGEMENT LEVEL, EDUCATION, LOCATION, AND ETHNICITY

Demographic factor	Knowledgeable about sustainability?				Knowledgeable about CSR?				Knowledgeable about CSP?			
	Yes		No		Yes		No		Yes		No	
	n	%	n	%	n	%	n	%	n	%	n	%
Gender												
male	34	81.0	8	19.0	33	78.6	9	21.4	19	54.2	23	54.8
female	24	75.0	8	25.0	14	45.2	17	54.8	8	25.0	24	75.0
Age												
18–29	14	82.4	3	17.6	9	56.3	7	43.8	7	41.2	10	58.8
30–45	16	64.0	9	36.0	16	64.0	9	36.0	7	28.0	18	72.0
45–60	23	88.5	3	11.5	18	69.2	8	30.8	11	42.3	15	57.7
60–75	5	83.3	1	16.7	5	83.3	1	16.7	2	33.3	4	66.7
Management level												
non-management	11	16.1	7	38.9	9	50.0	9	50.0	6	33.3	12	66.7
management	36	81.8	8	18.2	27	62.8	16	37.2	13	29.5	31	70.5
senior management	11	91.7	1	8.3	12	100	0	0.0	8	66.7	4	33.3
Education												
some college	2	66.7	1	33.3	2	66.7	1	33.3	1	33.3	2	66.7
undergraduate degree	6	75.0	2	25.0	6	75.0	2	25.0	4	50.0	4	50.0
graduate degree	33	82.5	7	17.5	27	67.5	13	32.5	13	32.5	27	67.5
doctorate degree	18	75.0	6	25.0	13	56.5	10	43.5	9	37.5	15	62.1
Location												
Africa	1	50.0	1	50.0	1	50.0	1	50.0	1	50.0	1	50.0
Asia	10	71.4	4	28.6	11	78.6	3	21.4	6	42.9	8	57.1
Europe	11	57.9	8	42.1	10	52.6	9	47.4	5	26.3	14	73.7
USA	33	94.3	2	5.7	25	71.4	10	28.6	13	37.1	22	62.9
Ethnicity												
Asian	11	73.3	4	26.7	11	73.3	4	26.7	6	40.0	9	60.0
Black	2	66.7	1	33.3	2	66.7	1	33.3	1	33.3	2	66.7
Hispanic	2	66.7	1	33.3	1	33.3	2	66.7	1	33.3	2	66.7
White	40	80.0	10	20.0	33	66.0	17	34.0	17	34.0	33	66.0

Note: N=81. Frequency is presented as percent of respondents selecting yes vs. no within each category.

TABLE 3.2   DESCRIPTIVE STATISTICS OF SATISFACTION WITH SOCIAL RESPONSIBILITY (SR) BY DEMOGRAPHIC FACTORS

Demographic factor	Satisfaction with social responsibility of country		Satisfaction with social responsibility of region		Satisfaction with social responsibility of local community	
	Mean	SD	Mean	SD	Mean	SD
Gender						
male	3.98	1.59	4.21	1.59	4.38	1.51
female	3.81	1.36	4.00	1.29	4.29	1.49
Total	3.91	1.48	4.12	1.46	4.34	1.49
Age						
18–29	3.94	1.35	3.81	1.38	4.00	1.32
30–45	3.92	1.47	4.28	1.37	4.60	1.50
45–60	3.88	1.73	4.19	1.65	4.31	1.69
60–75	4.17	0.98	4.33	1.37	4.67	0.82
Management level						
non-management	3.83	1.38	3.88	1.36	4.00	1.46
management	3.95	1.48	4.18	1.45	4.43	1.52
senior management	4.00	1.76	4.33	1.72	4.58	1.51
Education						
some college	3.67	1.53	3.67	1.16	4.33	1.53
undergraduate degree	4.50	1.20	4.38	1.30	5.00	1.41
graduate degree	3.83	1.52	4.18	1.48	4.28	1.47
doctorate degree	3.92	1.53	4.04	1.55	4.26	1.57
Location						
Africa	3.00	1.41	2.50*	0.71	4.50	2.12
Asia	4.07	1.33	3.93	1.49	3.93	1.39
Europe	3.89	1.60	4.22	1.40	4.28	1.49
USA	4.06	1.55	4.43	1.48	4.69	1.51
Ethnicity						
Asian	4.20*	1.37	4.07	1.53	4.07	1.44
Black	3.00	1.00	3.00	1.00	4.67	1.53
Hispanic	2.00	0.00	3.00	0.00	3.00	1.00
White	4.10	1.50	4.41	1.44	4.59	1.49

Note: Items scored 1 (very dissatisfied) – 7 (very satisfied); N = 81. *p <0.10 ANOVA test for difference in mean scores across demographic factor.

Furthermore, CSP should have been addressed specifically and separated from CSR and sustainability in the survey and interview questions.

In addition to assessing practitioner knowledge of sustainability and CSR, the survey assessed practitioner satisfaction with social responsibility of their country, region and local community. Table 3.2 presents descriptive statistics of satisfaction with social responsibility by demographic factors. As shown, the highest mean satisfaction with social responsibility occurred in the local community (mean = 4.34). This score reflects responses of "somewhat satisfied."

Social Responsibility Fragmentation in Competitiveness

Competitiveness is individually driven and relationally dependent. Therefore, how can corporations sustain social responsibility and remain competitive without reciprocation from local communities? As a result, competitiveness and social responsibility in CSR and sustainability is primarily economic and not socially driven because local communities do not reciprocate social competitiveness and social responsibility, thereby leaving corporations to compete and drive social responsibility economically. A practitioner in the 30–45 age group commented: "Competitiveness occurs when people perceive themselves to have self-efficacy and that must start at the individual." A practitioner in the 45–60 age group asks: "How does the individual fit in, when most of the CSR and competitiveness evaluations are at the macro level?" Personal responsibility may be a strong driver of environmental responsibility. Seventy-five percent of the practitioners in senior management and 63 percent in management determine that personal responsibility drives environmental responsibility in comparison to 40 percent in non-management that favor mandates and regulations over personal responsibility (Table 1.3). Most practitioners across management levels place stronger importance in individual competitiveness over community competitiveness. In addition, most practitioners with graduate and doctorate degrees agree that national competitiveness is dependent upon citizen responsibility in comparison to undergraduates and practitioners with some college (Table 1.2).

The data results in Tables 3.3, 3.4 and 3.5 reveal social fragmentation among individuals, corporations and local communities. Furthermore, most practitioners as local citizens have low corporate trust (Table 1.4). However, according to the practitioners, corporations are dependent upon local citizens' competitiveness to increase national competitiveness. A large number of practitioners across age groups agree that competition is good. It stimulates people to work hard and develop new ideas. How much should companies take responsibility when local communities can participate sporadically? Furthermore, income and poverty driven social responsibility limits crucial reciprocation from local communities for effective social responsibility with corporations and governments. Therefore, why is society demanding social responsibility from corporations and not in the local communities? Are local communities more socially responsible than corporations? Does society support different standards for local communities and corporations? (Windsor, 2001).

Most practitioners across management levels favor money and work over than local communities (Table 1.6). In addition, most practitioners in the 45–60 age group favor economic growth over protecting the environment. Since most practitioners fall within this age group, this impacts how the population views the importance and ranking of the three domains in CSR and sustainability (Table 1.5). Furthermore, the results suggest insight into CSR and sustainability discipline fragmentation where the economic domain leads, followed by the environmental domain and lastly the social domain. It is important to note that most practitioners agree that sustainability and CSR are dependent upon competitiveness. Since competitive advantage is defined as an economic driven phenomenon in CSR within the literature, this is the primary reason competitiveness is not defined within a social responsibility context of CSR and sustainability. It is noteworthy that human evolution and culturally adaptive systems are competing and strategically played in human-environment systems. Therefore, societal progress and competitiveness should be a component of CSR and sustainability to reveal contending and unequal social responsibility among local communities, governments and corporations.

Seven CSR and Sustainability Fragmentation Challenges

Seven CSR and sustainability challenges emerged from the data results. The seven challenges are selection bias, dependency on global and nationally recognized CSR and sustainability reporting tools, role of individuals, social responsibility knowledge fragmentation, social fragmentation, discipline fragmentation and cultural fragmentation (Tables 3.3–3.7).

CSR AND SUSTAINABILITY FRAGMENTATION CHALLENGE ONE: SELECTION BIAS

The first challenge is based upon numerous practitioners' responses describing the right people, right partnerships, right leadership and the right mindset for social responsibility in CSR and sustainability. Based on the data analyzed, CSR and sustainability initiatives are not dependent upon external social pressures. However, varieties of reciprocal societal standards must be monitored by corporations for implementation and growth of business CSR activities due to "associated erosion and dismantling of institutionalized social solidarity" (Kinderman, 2010). Despite corporate and government efforts to engage with local communities, "some places are not destined for greatness," "not fully engaged US public local communities" and have the "wrong mindset of 'this is good enough'" or in "survival mode." Nevertheless, one practitioner in the government prefers "impact and not monitoring to serve local communities instead of demanding progress and advancement." Therefore,

> selection bias warrants examination of a preferred ontology within "anthropogenic change" and "clarification of the relationships among different normative goals and identification of potential conflicts and trade-offs, including an ethical critique, with respect to the norm of justice, of individual preferences and claims from which criteria of efficiency are constructed. (Baumgartner and Quaas, 2010: 448)

CSR AND SUSTAINABILITY FRAGMENTATION CHALLENGE TWO: DEPENDENCY ON GLOBAL AND NATIONALLY RECOGNIZED CSR AND SUSTAINABILITY REPORTING TOOLS

The second challenge is based on practitioners' answers on monitoring social responsibility, social performance, creating CSR and sustainability reports, measuring CSR and sustainability and audits with mandate and regulation driven CSR and sustainability initiatives and strategies. Social construction is a driver of making social ordering legal. Thus, it can be argued that a wide variance in CSR reporting is a result of selected and broad preferences of CSR terms and concepts among corporations, governments, local communities and other stakeholders. Schaltegger (2012) suggests that sustainability reporting should move beyond communication projects to strategically establish a process of organizational learning and development. Since global reporting social preferences are heterogeneous, some partiality is inevitable. Moreover, some of the qualitative stratified data is homogenous across categories but heterogeneous within a category. This may be a result of global reporting standards instead of specific industry sector differentiation and best practice. Many corporations are reporting their social activities, but it is difficult to determine real progress or performance due to an under-developed social domain and socio-economic and societal well-being focus.

CSR AND SUSTAINABILITY FRAGMENTATION CHALLENGE THREE: ROLE OF INDIVIDUALS

The third challenge resulted in practitioners' responses such as "expert dependent," "individual," "voluntary" and lack of uncertainty in individuals about who is responsible in local communities, governments and corporations. The individual defines CSR and sustainability as socio-economic and natural environment driven, while responsibility and competitiveness is culturally interdependent and drives sustainability and CSR. Corporate social performance data are not included due to practitioners' significant uncertainty of what the concept means and its lack of practice within CSR and sustainability. CSR and sustainability strategies are self-interest driven with implicit social responsibility in individuals voluntarily meeting organizational moral expectations. Therefore, obtaining the common good in sustainability requires legitimate design of political institutions and operations (Blindheim, 2011). However, Hayek (1960) proposes there are many individual actors within society that need to be examined by gradual steps. Therefore, sustainability may constrain collective human behavior through individual social construction and prompt inquiry into whether sustainability is a collective outcome.

CSR AND SUSTAINABILITY FRAGMENTATION CHALLENGE FOUR: SOCIAL RESPONSIBILITY KNOWLEDGE FRAGMENTATION

The fourth challenge is based on practitioners' divided responses in social responsibility such as "stakeholder driven," "mandate driven," "no one is responsible," "all are responsible," "third party driven" and "environment driven" in determining responsibility among corporations, governments and local communities. Two practitioners from the 30–45 age group commented,

"I do not know exactly what it is" and "I am not sure what social responsibility means." Social responsibility is an ambiguous definition, driven implicitly and constructed in society by individual and group norms, values and beliefs. Social responsibility within business is a complex circumstance and is not focused solely on increasing profits and enhancing reputation management. Furthermore, society has its own organizations similar to business where differing values and beliefs create new organizations for ontological fit. Moreover, social and environmental performances are a source or condition for competitiveness (Valor, 2005).

CSR AND SUSTAINABILITY FRAGMENTATION CHALLENGE FIVE: SOCIAL FRAGMENTATION

The next challenge derived from practitioners' perceived and reality based risk management among local communities, governments and corporations. In general, social fragmentation is driven by formal and informal individual and group organization. For example, one practitioner frequently works with local communities and individuals in a "general state of informality with difficulties to establish traceability and lack of law enforcement." Practitioner answers include industry driven and scenario driven relationships. Moreover, uncertainty among the relationships of local communities, governments and corporations played an integral role in practitioners' answers. On the other hand, negative perceptions of corporations or a perceived strong corporate role with "government not helping" and local community driven strategies and initiatives depicted fragmented relationships. Many corporate practitioners monitor other corporations' CSR and sustainability social performance by what they say and what they do for learning and positioning. For example, social performance monitoring helps corporations to "think better and move quicker to better manage community risk and environmental risk." In monitoring social performance and attempting local community engagement, some practitioners in corporations recognize "the social is harder and it has to be local" and "set good examples for local communities to follow." On the other hand, one practitioner in the government sector suggested, "local communities can do it better and transform themselves," while others suggested "companies do social, not the government," "companies use social for themselves," it is "corporate driven" and "industry does more than government." Some practitioners in the government sector suggested that the reason the social is the least valued in

CSR and sustainability is due to the social is "not evident in media," "lack of headlines in media" and not "what are people paying attention to."

The focus of CSR and sustainability on societal well-being issues such as gender equality, equity, participation and social justice is sustaining social fragmentation due to differing societal ontological preferences. Value creation can be based upon inaccurate information among local communities, governments and corporations because individuals and groups create values that often conflict locally, regionally, nationally, and globally. Thus, social fragmentation and lack of trust between individuals and local communities and among governments, corporations and local communities provide insight into the strategic role of the individual in CSR and sustainability.

CSR AND SUSTAINABILITY FRAGMENTATION CHALLENGE SIX: DISCIPLINE FRAGMENTATION

CSR and sustainability are primarily a collaborative discipline balancing the economic, environment and social domains. However, practitioners' answers such as "isolated disciplines," "individual freedom driven," "personal driven," "local community driven," "government driven," "benefits driven," "industry driven," "economic and citizen driven," "environment driven," "management and leadership driven," "regulation driven," "following code of conduct trends," "uncertainty," "no voluntary choice for local community participation" and "need broad knowledge" resulted in discipline fragmentation. A common challenge shared by the practitioners across sectors and industries is the difficulty of social measurement. "We do not measure social performance," "no best practices, no good understanding of methodologies," "social measuring problems" and "what is the latest trend and where should we be heading? We do not integrate the social into business." Country and region groups resulted in greater emphasis on uncertainty and social fragmentation.

Discipline fragmentation within gender and sector or industry stratification results depicts a conflicting and diverse social responsibility focus within the economic, social and environmental domains, reflecting dependency upon pre-determined national and global recognized secondary sources for CSR and sustainability reporting tools in social responsibility initiatives and strategies. Nevertheless, CSR and sustainable development are primarily described as economic, environment and social dimensions (Littig and Grießier, 2005). However, it is questionable whether organizations can achieve success in all three dimensions simultaneously (Mersereau and Mottis, 2011).

Overall, societal welfare and well-being in the literature appears to be another way of establishing the social domain in CSR and sustainability and result in CSR and sustainability discipline fragmentation.

CSR AND SUSTAINABILITY FRAGMENTATION CHALLENGE SEVEN: CULTURAL FRAGMENTATION

The final challenge is based upon practitioner answers such as "local community limited boundaries and expectations," "corporate values driven," "locally driven," "societal needs/benefits driven," "monitor public and company values," "human rights challenges" and "differing mindsets."

Protocan and Mulej (2009), define social responsibility as interdependent human behavior including values, norms, ethics and culture that must be innovated. It can be argued that business values are simply a reflection of society's values. Therefore, corporations and local communities contain heterogeneous values and preferences that may be sporadically shared and diffused within competing cultural preferences.

The seven fragmentation challenges reveal individual selection bias within relationships and partnerships in CSR and sustainability among local communities, corporations and governments. This is often a result of differing expectations of competitiveness as corporations may have to rely more strongly on the economic domain of CSR and sustainability, especially if governments do not provide adequate incentives and regulations, and local communities do not reciprocate similar competitiveness expectations. In addition, the dependency upon global and nationally recognized CSR and sustainability reporting tools shapes individual, group and organizational CSR and sustainability strategies and practices that are not directly shared by governments and local communities due to lack of CSR and sustainability reporting of their reciprocating behavior and actions in CSR and sustainability with corporations. As a result, social, cultural and discipline fragmentation plays a critical role in sustaining a weak social domain and formal partnerships and relationships, thereby creating pretense of social responsibility among local communities, governments and corporations. Moreover, social responsibility knowledge fragmentation portrays that social responsibility is a vague and complex concept that contributes towards CSR and sustainability social responsibility dependency upon global reporting tools. Lastly, CSR and sustainability is primarily maintained by socially constructed reporting tools and preconstructed theories, methodologies and practices with a strong focus on the environmental and economic domains. As a result, deeper investigation of the role of society is warranted. Furthermore, social construction of the social domain in CSR and sustainability primarily highlights formal partnerships and alliances and does not delve into how the informal society culturally and socially constructing and impacting CSR and sustainability. Therefore, the informal society should be examined to better understand how the formal society and informal society is driving and reciprocating social responsibility and shaping the social domain in CSR and sustainability.

Stratification of Human and Social Bias

THE ROLE OF THE INDIVIDUAL

Seven fragmentation challenges are stratified as individual, gender, sector/industry and country/region groups. The challenges are presented by in Tables 3.3–3.7. Practitioners' significant codes, major patterns and final themes are highlighted by question number. CSR and sustainability is socio-economic and natural environment driven, while responsibility and competitiveness are culturally interdependent and drives sustainability and CSR. Corporate social performance in the quantitative and qualitative data was omitted due to participant knowledge fragmentation (Table 3.3). Question 4 in Section II resulted in practitioner uncertainty. This may be a result of the question wording or context.

THE ROLE OF GENDER

The female fragmentation challenges resulted in social fragmentation within local communities, governments and corporations (Table 3.4). Selection bias, discipline fragmentation and cultural fragmentation provide the results of the relationships between male practitioner codes and patterns to key final themes (Table 3.5). Discipline fragmentation within the female and male results depicts a conflicting and diverse social responsibility focus within the economic, social and environmental domains. It is no surprise that another key theme within male and female interview data codes and patterns is the dependency of corporations and governments to depend upon pre-determined national and global recognized secondary sources for CSR and sustainability reporting tools in social responsibility initiatives and strategies.

TABLE 3.3 RELATIONSHIP OF INDIVIDUAL PRACTITIONER CODES TO SEVEN FRAGMENTATION CHALLENGES

Question number	Individual practitioner code	Fragmentation challenge
Section I 1. How do you and others (local communities, governments and corporations) define sustainability, CSR, CSP, responsibility and competitiveness?	*Sustainability:* sustainable development CSR: corporate driven CSP: uncertain Responsibility: right mindset or mental state; mora focus; service Competitiveness: money; value sets; guiding principles; differentiation	Sustainability and CSR are socio-economic and natural environment driven CSP: not applicable Responsibility and competitiveness depict cultural fragmentation
2. How can corporations, governments and local communities create processes and patterns of shared responsibility and learning?	Right partnerships, groups and issues; change mindset; broad mindsets; culture driven; degrees of will; degrees of responsibility	Cultural fragmentation; selection bias
3. How do you measure Sustainability, CSR and CSP? What needs to be measured effectively to impact financial returns?	*Uncertain;* survey needs; privacy issue; social uncertainty	Dependency on global and national reporting tools; industry driven
4. Who determines responsibility among local communities, governments, and corporations? What is the difference in responsibility levels?	*All:* right people and leadership; stakeholder driven; mandate driven; None: third-party driven; environment driven	Selection bias; industry driven; social responsibility knowledge fragmentation
5. Please describe any gaps in the rule structures of sustainability, CSR and CSP that you have experienced.	Expert dependent; lack of uncertainty; voluntary; measuring inconsistency; laws not a solution; language gap	Individual driven
6. How do changing individual and group values and beliefs in your organization and society shape and impact sustainability, CSR and CSP?	Righ‑ mindset; corporation driven; isolated disciplines; individual freedom driven	Discipline fragmentation; selection bias
7. If there is no CSR, CSP and sustainability strategy, is there a vision or mission statement/corporate plan/other structure?	Right people and right mindset; trust pays off in the future; embeddedness; self-interest driven; synthesize social responsibility	Individually driven implicit social responsibility; selection bias
8. Has the organization's CSR, CSP and sustainability been audited/reviewed to evaluate its effectiveness?	34/111: no. Government driven internal and external reviews; third party (NGO, ISO, GRI)	Secondary sources pre-determined social responsibility reporting

9. How do you monitor social performance and social responsibility?	Surveys; relationship monitoring; industry driven specific criteria to determine change in local community	Dependency on global and nationally recognized reporting tools; social outputs emphasis
10. Do you receive training on CSR, CSP and sustainability? Is it effective for inter-organizational learning? Why or why not?	41/111: no. On the job; expert dependent; code of conduct guiding principles	Voluntary individual moral expectations focus
11. Do you report on CSR, CSP and sustainability? If so, what types of reports are published?	30/111: no. Reliance on secondary sources (GRI, ISO 26000, IR, DJSI)	Dependency on global and nationally recognized reporting tools
Section II 4. What are the legal, environmental, social, economic, technological, religious, cultural and political attributes of perceived and reality based risk management among local communities, government and corporations?	36/111: *uncertain*. Local community driven	Uncertainty; local community environment drives corporate involvement
7. Are local communities taking responsibility to work with your organization? Why or why not?	32/111: no. Need broad knowledge; local community mindset: limited local community boundaries and expectations	Cultural fragmentation

TABLE 3.4 RELATIONSHIP OF FEMALE PRACTITIONER CODES TO SEVEN FRAGMENTATION CHALLENGES

Question number	Significant code	Fragmentation challenges
Section I 4. Who determines responsibility among local communities, governments, and corporations? What is the difference in responsibility levels?	*All*: contextual; government and corporation driven; local community and corporation driven; locally driven; environment driven; industry partnerships driven	Industry strategy driven; Discipline fragmentation
6. How do changing individual and group values and beliefs in your organization and society shape and impact sustainability, CSR and CSP?	Personal driven; local community driven; government driven; management and leadership driven; dialogue driven	Discipline fragmentation
9. How do you monitor social performance and social responsibility?	*Uncertain*. Surveys; societal benefits driven; regulation driven	Dependency on national and global recognized reporting tools
Section II 4. What are the legal, environmental, social, economic, technological, religious, cultural and political attributes of perceived and reality based risk management among local communities, government, and corporations?	*Uncertain*. Industry driven; scenario driven relationships	Uncertainty; social fragmentation
7. Are local communities taking responsibility to work with your organization? Why or why not?	Negative perceptions of corporations; need local community voice heard; corporate driven; government not helping	Social fragmentation

TABLE 3.5   RELATIONSHIP OF MALE PRACTITIONER CODES TO SEVEN FRAGMENTATION CHALLENGES

Question number	Significant code	Fragmentation challenges
Section I 4. Who determines responsibility among local communities, governments, and corporations? What is the difference in responsibility levels?	*All*: self-interest driven *None*: mandate driven	Discipline fragmentation
6. How do changing individual and group values and beliefs in your organization and society shape and impact sustainability, CSR and CSP?	Corporation values driven; right mindset; individual driven	Cultural fragmentation; selection bias
9. How do you monitor social performance and social responsibility?	*Uncertain*. Surveys; relationship monitoring; pre-determined national and global social reporting tools	Dependency on national and globally recognized reporting tools
Section II 4. What are the legal, environmental, social, economic, technological, religious, cultural and political attributes of perceived and reality based risk management among local communities, government and corporations?	*Uncertain*. Societal needs understanding; locally driven	Uncertainty; discipline fragmentation
7. Are local communities taking responsibility to work with your organization? Why or why not?	Locally driven; government driven; limited local community boundaries and expectations; right mindset	Social and cultural fragmentation; selection bias

THE ROLE OF SECTOR/INDUSTRY

Sector/industry stratification resulted in similar fragmentation challenges in comparison to gender stratification with a greater emphasis on uncertainty and social fragmentation (Table 3.6).

TABLE 3.6   RELATIONSHIP OF SECTOR CODES TO SEVEN FRAGMENTATION CHALLENGES

Question number	Significant code	Fragmentation challenges
Section I 4. Who determines responsibility among local communities, governments and corporations? What is the difference in responsibility levels?	*Non-profit*: all *Public, agricultural*: all *Private, agricultural*: contextual *Private, chemical*: local community driven *Consumer products*: local community driven *Private, information technology*: industry partnerships *Public, federal, state and local government*: all; mandate driven; government driven	Discipline fragmentation; social fragmentation
6. How do changing individual and group values and beliefs in your organization and society shape and impact sustainability, CSR and CSP?	*Non-profit*: monitor public and company values *Public, agricultural*: individual driven *Private, agricultural*: right mindset; consistency of culture *Private, chemical*: corporate values and code of conduct driven *Consumer products*: corporate values and code-of-conduct driven *Private, information technology*: philanthropy; voluntary *Public, federal, state and local government*: right mindset; individual driven; government driven	Cultural fragmentation; social fragmentation; selection bias
9. How do you monitor social performance and social responsibility?	*Non-profit*: local community benefits driven; Corporation monitoring *Public, agricultural*: individual driven *Private, agricultural*: supply chain monitoring *Private, chemical*: set expectations *Consumer products*: set expectations *Private, information technology*: digital inclusion *Public, federal, state and local government*: benefits and self-interest driven; local community driven	Societal benefits driven within pre-determined national and global social reporting tools

TABLE 3.6   RELATIONSHIP OF SECTOR CODES TO SEVEN FRAGMENTATION CHALLENGES (*CONCLUDED*)

Question number	Significant code	Fragmentation challenges
Section II 4. What are the legal, environmental, social, economic, technological, religious, cultural and political attributes of perceived and reality based risk management among local communities, government and corporations?	*Non-profit: uncertain* *Public, agricultural: uncertain* *Private, agricultural: uncertain* *Private, chemical: uncertain* *Consumer products:* corporate values and code-of-conduct driven *Private, information technology:* scenario driven *Public, federal, state and local government: uncertain.* Local community driven; corporation dependent	Uncertainty; discipline fragmentation
7. Are local communities taking responsibility to work with your organization? Why or why not?	*Non-profit:* local community partnership outreach *Public, agricultural:* no voluntary choice; need opportunities *Private, agricultural:* right mindset; local community role *Private, chemical:* dialogue *Consumer products:* human rights challenges *Private, information technology: Uncertain.* Local community participation *Public, federal, state and local government:* local community driven; need broad knowledge; government driven	Social and cultural fragmentation; selection bias

THE ROLE OF LOCATION

Country/region stratification results were similar to fragmentation challenges in the sector/industry stratification (Table 3.7). The similarity among sectors, industries and country/region may be an outcome of the dependency of national and global social reporting tools. It is interesting to note that practitioner responses across categories were homogenous, while practitioner responses within categories were heterogeneous.

TABLE 3.7   RELATIONSHIP OF COUNTRY/REGION CODES TO SEVEN FRAGMENTATION CHALLENGES

Question number	Significant code	Fragmentation challenges
Section I 4. Who determines responsibility among local communities, governments and corporations? What is the difference in responsibility levels?	*Europe*: formal coordination *India / Kerala*: government and corporation driven *Netherlands, Amsterdam*: market and stakeholder driven *Switzerland, Vevey*: use third party *Switzerland*: all *United Kingdom, London*: all *United Kingdom*: nationally driven *United Kingdom, Newcastle*: market driven *USA, Mid-Atlantic*: stakeholder driven; corporation driven; local community driven; mandate driven *USA, North East*: local community driven *USA, Pacific*: contextual *USA, Central*: self-determination and right people and leadership *USA, Southeast*: natural environment driven; citizen driven	Social and discipline fragmentation
6. How do changing individual and group values and beliefs in your organization and society shape and impact sustainability, CSR and CSP?	*Europe*: framework dependent *India / Kerala*: government driven *Netherlands, Amsterdam*: integration of organization values *Switzerland, Vevey*: right mindset *Switzerland*: corporation driven *United Kingdom, London*: right mindset *United Kingdom*: credibility *United Kingdom, Newcastle*: champions in organization *USA, Mid-Atlantic*: differing mindsets; right mindset; individual driven; isolated disciplines *USA, North East*: follow code of conduct trends *USA, Pacific*: individual driven *USA, Central*: education *USA, Southeast*: right collaboration	Cultural fragmentation; social fragmentation; selection bias
9. How do you monitor social performance and social responsibility?	*Europe*: national and global reporting tools *India / Kerala*: socio-economic driven *Netherlands, Amsterdam*: human rights and dialogue *Switzerland, Vevey*: global reporting tools *Switzerland*: management evaluation system *United Kingdom, London*: national and global reporting tools *United Kingdom*: national and global reporting tools *United Kingdom, Newcastle*: environment driven *USA, Mid-Atlantic*: national and global reporting tools; corporation driven; persuasion *USA, North East*: national and global reporting tools *USA, Pacific*: national and global reporting tools *USA, Central*: corporation driven *USA, Southeast*: supply chain, societal benefits and labor monitoring	Societal benefits driven within pre-determined national and global social reporting tools

TABLE 3.7   RELATIONSHIP OF COUNTRY/REGION CODES TO SEVEN FRAGMENTATION CHALLENGES (*CONCLUDED*)

Question number	Significant code	Fragmentation challenges
9. How do you monitor social performance and social responsibility?	*Europe*: national and global reporting tools *India / Kerala*: socio-economic driven *Netherlands, Amsterdam*: human rights and dialogue *Switzerland, Vevey*: global reporting tools *Switzerland*: management evaluation system *United Kingdom*: national and global reporting tools *United Kingdom, London*: national and global reporting tools *United Kingdom, Newcastle*: environment driven *USA, Mid-Atlantic*: national and global reporting tools; corporation driven; persuasion *USA, North East*: national and global reporting tools *USA, Pacific*: national and global reporting tools *USA, Central*: corporation driven *USA, Southeast*: supply chain, societal benefits, and labor monitoring	Societal benefits driven within pre-determined national and global social reporting tools
Section II 4. What are the legal, environmental, social, economic, technological, religious, cultural and political attributes of perceived and reality-based risk management among local communities, government and corporations?	*Europe* – Uncertainty *India / Kerala* – Uncertainty *Netherlands, Amsterdam* – Uncertainty *Switzerland, Vevey* – Continuous improvement; Expert dependent *Switzerland* – Uncertainty *United Kingdom* – Benefits driven *United Kingdom, London* – Scenario driven *United Kingdom, Newcastle* - Uncertainty *USA, Mid-Atlantic* – Local community driven; Uncertainty; Dialogue *USA, North East* – Uncertainty *USA, Pacific* – Reputation Management *USA, Central* – Local relationships driven *USA, Southeast* – Economic and citizen driven	Uncertainty; discipline fragmentation
7. Are local communities taking responsibility to work with your organization? Why or why not?	*Europe*: limited local community boundaries and expectations *India / Kerala*: government driven *Netherlands, Amsterdam*: facilitator role *Switzerland, Vevey*: right mindset *Switzerland*: local community engagement guidelines *United Kingdom*: uncertain *United Kingdom, London*: local community driven *United Kingdom, Newcastle*: local government driven *USA, Mid-Atlantic*: uncertain. Local community education and outreach *USA, North East*: corporation driven; government not helpful *USA, Pacific*: uncertain *USA, Central*: uncertain *USA, Southeast*: uncertain	Social and cultural fragmentation; uncertainty; selection bias

The triangulation of qualitative data-analysis techniques provided validation for the coding and patterns in the web-based survey text and interview data final themes. In this section of the chapter, secondary sources are combined with the qualitative data analysis techniques and integrate several strengths of positivist and interpretive approaches to increase the credibility of the data results. Most practitioners utilize some form of CSR and sustainability reporting and are dependent upon the major CSR and sustainability global and national reporting tools for competitive advantage. However, it is beyond the scope of this research study to examine several of the leading global, national and industry focused CSR and sustainability reporting tools. The Global Reporting Initiative (GRI) is the primary CSR and sustainability reporting tools that were employed and compared by the practitioners followed with some practitioners moving towards Integrated Reporting (IR). For these reasons, the GRI and IR will be selected as secondary sources for triangulation of qualitative data results.

The GRI is organized into three categories—economic, social and environmental—with the social category described as labor practices and decent work, human rights, society and product responsibility (GRI, 2014). Since this research study highlights and examines the social domain with less emphasis on the economic and environmental domains, the GRI's society performance indictors will be compared with the qualitative data results. The society performance indicators include local communities, anti-corruption, public policy, anti-competitive behavior, compliance, supplier assessment for impacts on society and grievance mechanisms for impacts on society. Integrated Reporting (IR) consists of an integrated process to create value sustainably within a sliced framework of financial statements, governance reports and sustainability reports. The social in IR is broadly defined as social capital and social matters engaging communities, stakeholders and other social networks for societal well-being (Integrated Reporting, 2013).

It is evident that the social domains in GRI and IR are broadly defined for corporations to include social issues within the organization's industry and CSR or sustainability strategy. Comparing the qualitative themes with the IR and GRI, it can be concluded that the dependency of CSR and sustainability pre-determined reporting tools may shape the practitioners definition of social as socio-economic and well-being responsibility initiatives. Furthermore, knowledge and discipline fragmentation may be the results of broad reporting frameworks with unclear and varied CSR and sustainability frameworks and fuzzy social responsibility global and national reporting tools.

The data results demonstrate that governments and local communities are interdependent for social responsibility and competitiveness with age and gender as influential factors. Overall, the quantitative and qualitative major patterns and themes resulted in higher government trust than corporate trust with the individual playing a stronger role than collaborative relationships. Personal trust is essential to CSR and sustainability and may be a driver of selection bias and cultural fragmentation within CSR and sustainability. National competitiveness is dependent upon local competitiveness. Corporations are dependent upon local competitiveness and local communities are dependent upon governments for social responsibility and competitiveness. Furthermore, the strong socio-economic and societal well-being emphasis of practitioners and reporting tools pervades attitudes and perceptions of CSR and sustainability resulting in the economic domain leading, followed by natural environment and lastly the social domain. Moreover, money and work are more important than local communities.

CHAPTER 4

The Relationships of Governments, Local Communities and Corporations in Social Responsibility

Governments, corporations and local communities have the potential to impact each other positively and negatively in CSR and sustainability. Critically examining CSR and sustainability for inappropriate and potentially false representation of social responsibility among local communities, governments and corporations is warranted due to a plethora of varying definitions, theories, methods and social constructions of CSR and sustainability. This chapter will discuss the roles of governments, corporations and local communities in social responsibility and competitiveness and how governments, corporations and local communities impact each other in CSR and sustainability with a discussion of personal trust and individual accomplishment in social responsibility. A social responsibility model describes ways to manage tensions between relational risk and the common good.

Practitioner Views in Government, Corporation and Local Community Relationships

It is important to understand the practitioners' demographic characteristics as employees, middle and senior management from corporations and federal, state and local governments and their self-reported views about CSR and sustainability. The practitioners' demographic characteristics from the survey are briefly described for understanding how the data results contribute to establishing impacts among corporations, local communities and governments in CSR and sustainability.

TABLE 4.1   DEMOGRAPHIC CHARACTERISTICS OF WEB-BASED SURVEY STUDY SAMPLE STRATIFIED BY GENDER, AGE, MANAGEMENT LEVEL, EDUCATION, LOCATION, AND ETHNICITY

Demographic factor	Total		Male		Female	
	n	%	n	%	n	%
Gender						
male	42	51.9	42	100.0	–	–
female	32	39.5	–	–	32	100.0
no response	7	8.6	–	–	–	–
Age						
18–29	17	21.0**	8	19.0**	8	25.00**
30–45	25	30.9	11	26.2	14	43.8
45–60	26	32.1	18	42.9	8	25.0
60–75	6	7.4	5	11.9	1	3.1
no response	7	8.6	0	0.0	1	3.1
Management level						
non-management	18	22.2	9	21.4	9	28.1
management	44	54.3	26	61.9	18	56.2
senior management	12	14.8**	7	16.7**	4	12.5**
no response	7	8.6	0	0.0	1	3.1
Education						
some college	3	3.7**	2	4.8**	1	3.1**
undergraduate degree	8	9.9	6	14.3	2	6.2
graduate degree	40	49.4	18	42.9	21	65.6
doctorate degree	24	29.6	16	38.1	8	25.0
no response	6	7.4	0	0.0	0	0.0
Location						
Africa	2	2.5**	2	4.8**	0	0.0**
Asia	14	17.3	12	28.6	1	3.1
Europe	19	23.4	6	14.4	13	40.6
USA	35	43.2	20	47.6	15	46.9
no response	11	13.6	2	4.8	3	9.4
Ethnicity						
Asian	15	18.5**	13	31.0**	1	3.1**
Black	3	3.7	2	4.8	1	3.1
Hispanic	3	3.7	1	2.4	2	6.2
White	50	61.7	24	57.1	26	81.2
no response	10	12.3	2	4.8	2	6.2

Notes: N=81; N male = 42; N female = 32; N no response = 7. **p<0.01 Chi-square test for equality of distribution.

TABLE 4.2   WEB-BASED SURVEY PARTICIPANTS BY PRIVATE INDUSTRY AND LOCATION

Industry	Location	Male		Female		Total	
		n	%	n	%	n	%
Agricultural	USA	9	36.0	6	54.5	15	41.7
	Europe	6	24.0	0	0.0	6	16.7
Consumer goods and services	USA	2	8.0	0	0.0	2	5.6
Chemical	USA	2	8.0	0	0.0	2	5.6
	Europe	0	0.0	1	9.1	1	2.8
Forestry	USA	0	0.0	1	9.1	1	2.8
Information technology	USA	1	4.0	1	9.1	2	5.6
	Europe	0	0.0	1	9.1	1	2.8
	India	4	16.0	0	0.0	4	11.1
Industrial	USA	0	0.0	1	9.1	1	2.8
Office Supplies	USA	1	4.0	0	0.0	1	2.8

Notes: N = 36; N male = 25; N female = 11.

TABLE 4.3   WEB-BASED SURVEY PARTICIPANTS BY PUBLIC INDUSTRY AND LOCATION

Industry	Location	Male		Female		Total	
		n	%	n	%	n	%
Agriculture	USA	15	42.9	5	22.7	20	35.1
Natural environment	USA	11	31.4	15	68.2	26	45.6
	Europe	2	5.7	0	0.0	2	3.5
Energy	USA	2	5.7	0	0.0	2	3.5
State	India	2	5.7	1	4.5	3	5.3
Forestry	USA	1	2.9	0	0.0	1	1.8
Labor	USA	1	2.9	1	4.5	2	3.5
Business development	India	1	2.9	0	0.0	1	1.8

Notes: N = 57; male N = 35; female N = 22.

TABLE 4.4   WEB-BASED SURVEY PARTICIPANTS BY LOCAL INDUSTRY AND LOCATION

Industry	Location	Male		Female		Total	
		n	%	n	%	N	%
Business development	USA	1	33.3	2	33.3	3	33.3
Forestry	USA	1	33.3	0	0.0	1	11.1
Natural environment	USA	0	0.0	1	16.7	1	11.1
International natural environment	USA	0	0.0	2	33.3	2	22.2
	Europe	0	0.0	1	16.7	1	11.1
Local government	Europe	1	33.3	0	0.0	1	11.1

Notes: N = 9; N male = 3; N = female 6.

As shown in Table 4.1, age, management level, education, location and ethnicity but not gender had wide differences. The largest group of practitioners were in the 45–60 age range (32.1%), at management level (54.3%), with graduate degrees (49.4%), in the USA (43.2%) and white (61.7%). Males within the 45–60 age group included senior management and management. Senior management is defined as the C-suite and management is defined as department heads or managers of a department. Most practitioners in management held graduate and doctorate degrees with some college education, while primarily non-management practitioners held an undergraduate degree, and most senior management practitioners received some college education. Practitioners in senior management and management were primarily male with more females in non-management.

Demographic characteristics are also presented for the practitioners who were interviewed (Tables 4.2–4.4). Demographic characteristics for the interviewees are presented as frequency distribution of gender, location and public, private and local industry type.

Role of Corporations in Social Responsibility and Competitiveness

Three hypotheses are briefly discussed for understanding how the formation and data results lead to a social responsibility model among corporations, local communities and governments. The first hypothesis was: "Is social responsibility within local communities dependent upon corporations to increase local, regional and national competitive advantage?"

TABLE 4.5   LINEAR REGRESSION RESULTS FOR HYPOTHESIS 1

Independent variable	B	SE	T	p
Local communities require accountability from corporations for social responsibility and local community competitiveness	0.285	0.127	2.24	0.028*
Age	−0.221	−0.108	−2.05	0.044*
Management level	0.080	0.156	0.52	0.608

Notes: R-square = 0.118; F3,71 = 3.04, p = 0.035. * p < 0.05 linear regression test for significance of independent variable as a predictor of increase in local, national and regional competitive advantage.

This question was tested using the inferential statistic linear regression in which the dependent variable, "national competitiveness is dependent upon local community competitiveness," was regressed on the independent variable, "local communities require accountability from corporations for social responsibility and local community competitiveness." Additionally, age and management level were included in the regression analysis covariates. As shown in Table 4.5, the independent variable is a significant predictor of the dependent variable at the p < 0.05 level of significance. This result suggests the null hypothesis can be rejected and the hypothesis has statistical support. Accordingly, when local communities are held accountable for social responsibility by corporations, then local, national and regional competitive advantage is likely to increase.

Role of Governments in Social Responsibility and Competitiveness

Hypothesis 2 was "Are local communities dependent upon governments for social responsibility and increasing national and global competitive advantage?" This question was tested using the inferential statistic linear regression in which the dependent variable, "national competitiveness is dependent upon local community competitiveness," was regressed on the independent variable, "government is responsible for local communities' responsibility and competitiveness." Additionally, age and management level were included in the regression analysis covariates. As shown in Table 4.6, the independent variable is a significant predictor of the dependent variable at the p < 0.05 level of significance. This result suggests the null hypothesis can be rejected and the hypothesis has statistical support.

TABLE 4.6   LINEAR REGRESSION RESULTS FOR HYPOTHESIS 2

Independent variable	B	SE	T	p
Government is responsible for social responsibility and competitiveness at the local level	0.209	0.088	2.39	0.020*
Age	−0.173	0.117	−1.48	−0.144
Management level	0.147	0.096	1.54	0.129

Notes: R-square = 0.103; F3,71 = 4.62; p = 0.013.* p < 0.05 linear regression test for significance of independent variable as a predictor of increase in local, national and regional competitive advantage.

Accordingly, when governments hold local communities accountable for social responsibility and competitiveness, then local, national and regional competitive advantage is likely to increase.

The descriptive statistics indicate most practitioners agree government is responsible for local communities' responsibility and competitiveness, and trust government more than corporations with the exception of practitioners in the 18–29 age group and senior management. Governments are incorporating CSR codes of conduct to reduce costs and efficiencies as a component of their national competitiveness strategies (Petkoski and Twose, 2003). However, should local communities be the driver of social responsibility without oversight from the government?

Many practitioners agreed that government should hold local communities responsible for local communities' social responsibility and competitiveness in the descriptive statistics. Senior management and management agree, while non-management disagree that the government is responsible for local communities' responsibility and competitiveness. This may be a result of how most practitioners view a greater role in personal trust and individual competitiveness over community competitiveness for increasing competitiveness and social responsibility.

Role of Local Communities in Social Responsibility and Competitiveness

Hypothesis 3 was "Are governments and corporations dependent upon local communities for social responsibility that results in increasing local, national and regional competitive advantage?" This question was tested using the inferential statistic linear regression in which the dependent variable,

TABLE 4.7   LINEAR REGRESSION RESULTS FOR HYPOTHESIS 3

Independent variable	B	SE	T	p
Local communities require accountability from government for social responsibility and local community competitiveness	0.348	0.127	2.74	0.008**
Age	−0.231	0.105	−2.21	0.031*
Management level	0.038	0.153	0.25	0.805

Notes: R-square = 0.164; F3,71 = 4.62; p = 0.006. * p < 0.05 linear regression test for significance of independent variable as a predictor of increase in local, national and regional competitive advantage. ** p < 0.01 linear regression test for significance of independent variable as a predictor of increase in local, national and regional competitive advantage.

"national competitiveness is dependent upon local community competitiveness," was regressed on the independent variable, "local communities require accountability from government for social responsibility and local community competitiveness." Additionally, age and management levels were included in the regression analysis covariates. As shown in Table 4.7, the independent variable is a significant predictor of the dependent variable at the p < .01 level of significance. This result suggests the null hypothesis can be rejected and the hypothesis has statistical support. Accordingly, when local communities hold government and corporations accountable for social responsibility and competitiveness, then local, national and regional competitive advantage is likely to increase.

Ethnicity and gender play an important role in determining who will hold local communities accountable for national competitiveness thereby increasing the potential of local, national and regional competitive advantage. Overall, social responsibility within CSR and sustainability in the local community is most significant in comparison to the country level and regional levels of practitioners' responses. This may be a result of social spatial perceptions among practitioners living in local places that are familiar and considered home to the practitioners in depicting social desirability in comparison to geographic areas that are less familiar (Table 3.2).

Practitioners across age groups and management levels reveal some uncertainty in trusting local businesses with greater trust in government than corporations in the descriptive statistics. Most gender and age groups agree that national competitiveness is dependent upon local community competitiveness.

It could be argued that because local communities are dependent upon corporations for wealth creation, they disregard social responsibility from local communities to corporations as unnecessary. Moreover, the government also plays a role in the lack of social responsibility from local communities to corporations through creation and incentives within regulations, laws and policies.

Individual Accomplishment and Personal Trust as a Key Driver in Social Responsibility and Competitiveness

An alternative hypothesis emerged from the quantitative data results revealing personal trust and individual accomplishment as primary drivers in social responsibility. Personal trust and individual accomplishment drive social responsibility and competitiveness with most practitioners concurring, "citizens have the same responsibility as government and corporations for social responsibility and national competitiveness" (Table 1.3).

Most practitioners across management levels place greater emphasis on personal trust than relational trust in CSR and sustainability. For example, practitioners answered neither true or false for developing trust within their local communities. Moreover, age was a significant covariate in the hypotheses 1 and 3 regression analyses and was not significant in hypothesis 2. This implies that younger people may be more accountable and more interested and focused on social responsibility than older age groups. Furthermore, most practitioners across management levels trust their local businesses and their neighborhood somewhat in comparison to trusting their family completely, and trust corporations and governments somewhat in comparison to trusting their family completely (Table 1.4).

Trust was found to be a significant implicit contributing factor in selecting partnerships in CSR and sustainability. Most practitioners view the social as socio-economics, social welfare and social well-being with society defined as varying stakeholders. Moreover, the economic domain is ranked first, followed by the environmental domain and lastly the social domain. The data results and literature draw out the need for social development beyond socio-economics in CSR and sustainability. Previous research also identified competitiveness in CSR and sustainability as relationally driven while the practitioners highlighted that it is the individual that plays a stronger role in driving competition in CSR and sustainability.

The data results for the variable trust depict most practitioners embedding particular trust over general trust. General trust is based upon permitting some trust of unknown others, while particular trust is found in familiar networks (Luo, 2005). As a result, there is discipline fragmentation and cultural fragmentation between practitioners' local community trust and local community competitiveness. "Creating the generalized trust needed for social cooperation is not simply a matter of getting people together, they must start with a high level of generalized trust" (Uslaner and Conley, 2003: p. 356). Relational trust is dependent upon history-dependent processes (Kramer, 1999) and should be fostered by genuine motives and trust (Phillips, 1997; Swift, 2001) within cultural history. However, stakeholder unsuitability (Wood and Jones, 1995) reveals challenges for sustaining relationships among local communities, governments and corporations. This may be a result of trust as a meso contextual concept, integrating micro and macro social processes (House, Rousseau and Thomas-Hunt, 1995). Furthermore, "trust is not a behavior or a choice, but an underlying psychological condition that can cause or result from such actions" (Rousseau et al., 1998: 395). Particular trust reduces diversity and increased diversity creates challenges in trust formation (Weick, 1987).

Social Responsibility is Individually Driven but Socially Determined and Constructed

This section will present a social responsibility model that is created from the quantitative and qualitative data findings (Figure 4.1) and the reciprocation of informal and formal societies in the social domain system of CSR and sustainability (Figure 4.2). The most suitable methodology for investigating the theoretical foundations of social responsibility among corporations, governments and local communities is a descriptive model design. The social responsibility model embeds itself within the social domain of CSR and sustainability and depicts the relationships between adjustments at the micro and macro levels with emergent properties at the meso level among individuals, local communities, governments and corporations.

The descriptive model design in Figure 4.1 is inductive, dynamic and normative and is based on analysis of data results for hypothesis 2. This model differs from previous CSR and sustainability models for determining social performance by not conforming to existing conventional socio-economic and socio-environment narrative forms. The model considers regularities that are

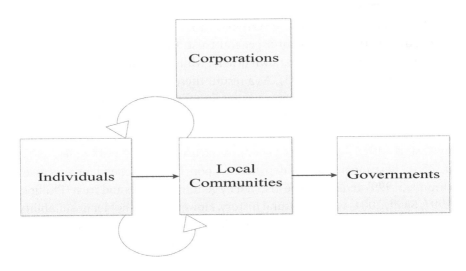

FIGURE 4.1 SOCIAL RESPONSIBILITY MODEL
Source: Author.

not explained by current CSR and sustainability models, thereby focusing on relational risk, trust, values and beliefs and competitiveness among individuals, local communities, governments and corporations within the social domain of CSR and sustainability. The model is not an optimal determination. Rather, it incorporates a normative view of hypothesis 2 and undeclared and declared assumptions and qualitative data results for evaluating and understanding social performance. The model's assumptions acknowledge that hard relational boundaries create fuzzy, complex shifting paradigms among individuals, local communities, governments and corporations in social responsibility and social performance. Furthermore in an effort to explain change and invite performative discourse, the model makes some assumptions for underlying social domain causes as found in a formal and informal society.

The data results show that social responsibility is driven by individuals in local communities within formal and informal societies that create a common good tension among local communities, governments and corporations. The individuals and local communities are reciprocal while the government is responsible for local communities' social responsibility and competitiveness, leaving corporations disjointed. Generally, sustainability and CSR models include individuals and communities as stakeholders. This is problematic to address stakeholders as society as it depicts society as a combined bulk category. Instead, it is necessary to examine relationships between specific stakeholders and to include a government domain (Thiel, 2010) in the social responsibility model. The informal and formal societies shape the social domain and are both strategically driven and are competing on varying levels within the heterarchy across time and space. Moreover, the social domain is based upon how social phenomena are influenced by beliefs, some true and some false, thereby creating different results. The model's design and methodology considers incomplete knowledge, imperfection of values and perception biases for explaining emergent social phenomena. The example of social responsibility reciprocation in the model identifies some causal responsibility in complex social systems by evaluating the data results presuppositions of trust, values and beliefs and competitiveness that are dependent upon the sample population's conception of them. If social responsibility is primarily verified through individual responsibility and social norms, legal compliance is deficient. Shared information is considered more valuable and valid than unshared information for group decision-making (Hogg and Reid, 2006). Society's unwillingness to evaluate its certainty and accepted assumptions within mainstream media are found throughout the social and common good panorama. Or, perhaps it is a result of "informational cascades" where individuals "ignore their own information and imitate the behavior or other, supposedly better informed agents," creating further cascading of suppressed information (Gale, 1996: p. 618).

The gap between corporations and governments can also be a consequence of non-governmental organizations resource approach and not relational approaches to informal social processes in local community advocacy (Thiel, 2013). The quantitative and qualitative data results show that individuals and local communities reciprocate trust and are dependent upon governments for social responsibility with a gap in the relationships with corporations. Trust among individuals, local communities and governments are greater than corporate trust. In the social responsibility model, society is equitable in institutional formal forms, but not within informal forms, because this is something most corporations do not capture. And, it is the informal society that drives social responsibility and competitiveness. The formal society includes a system of rules, sanctions and laws for individual and social cooperation that are inadequate and require monitoring of self-interest (Peachey and Lerner, 1981). Further to this, "people implicitly associate the law with competitiveness and that activating the law can have adverse effects on interpersonal trust and cooperation" (Callan et al., 2010: p. 33).

The social domain consists of formal and informal relationships between individuals and groups that are distinguished from formal and informal institutions. Societal environment is presented as formal and informal organization. Society's decisions are influenced and strongly managed by the informal in comparison to the formal society reciprocating at varying levels between the informal society and formal society. The model's framework acknowledges a scope of uncertainty within the borders of the problem. Broad reciprocation among individuals, local communities, governments and corporations can have multiple and unexpected consequences that are not explicit within the model's frameworks and components. Underlying reasons for the social responsibility fragmentation are assumed based upon values and cultural preferences in an informal and formal society. However, values can be misleading because people will adopt strategies for values that appear vital for social betterment while retaining their conflicting societal values in different contexts and conditions, thereby resulting in false and misleading perceptions of social progress and human development. Therefore, values are heterarchial and are in a constant state of flux.

An informal and formal society provides tension to the common good resulting in gaps between corporations, local communities and individuals, thereby leading to decreased societal competitiveness, social progress and higher dependency upon governments for social responsibility. The latent strategy of reciprocal relational force within individuals and groups in the informal and formal societies evolve and shape social responsibility among corporations, governments and local communities (Figure 4.2). The informal society may appear disorganized, but through its temporal, spatial and permanent relationships, the informal society drives forces of change geographically and can morph cultures for reputation management.

The lack of local communities reciprocating social responsibility to corporations is twofold. First, it is potentially due to individuals driving social responsibility through self-enforcing social norms within local communities and local communities sustaining dependency upon governments for its own social responsibility and competitiveness. Second, it is may be due to an under-developed social domain. In an effort to develop the social domain, a formal and informal society depicts the environment that intersects individuals and groups conditionally and in relationally complex ways. Critical evaluation warrants social responsibility's underlying processes within a larger social structural context. Furthermore, the use of the term "social" can lead to the evasion of responsibility because it fails to address the roles of individuals and local communities in what may be considered the formal and informal society of the social domain within CSR and sustainability. Formal society consists of socio-institutions, signed and contractual partnerships and collaboration

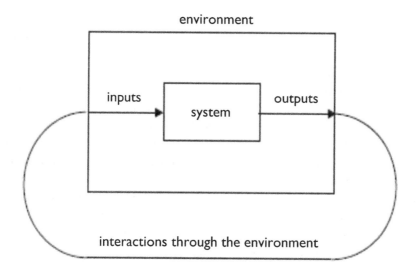

FIGURE 4.2 RECIPROCATION OF INFORMAL AND FORMAL SOCIETIES IN THE SOCIAL DOMAIN SYSTEM

Source: Author.

with various stakeholders, while the informal society can be described as individuals and local communities that are always interacting heterogeneously and homogenously within and around the formal society creating a strategic culture that is hidden by the formal society. Since individual preferences are not homogenous, not all preferences will be incorporated into the formal society. However, they will be sustained in the informal society. Thus, the greater the threat to the local community, the greater the selection bias (Van Knippenberg, 1984). Likewise, the greater the selection bias in a local community, the greater the threat to sustaining genuine democracy to all cultures. Consequently, the informal society should be monitored and not left unattended and perceived as innocent individuals and local communities because it is the informal society that may constrain advancement and societal progress. This suggests that the social domain in CSR and sustainability as a unified reporting practice is misunderstood. Furthermore, culture is part of human biology in human systems (Durham, 1991; Henrich, 2004). The prisoner's dilemma depicts reciprocity strategies that provide benefits to individuals who repeatedly reciprocate may be selected to ensure repeated reciprocation (Axelrod, 1984). This implies that in order to better understand social progress and self-enforcing social norms and collective collusion, the social processes integrating the examination of how behavioral information is communicated across generations (Henrich, 2004) requires examination of the informal and formal society for potential reputational harm.

The data findings show that CSR and sustainability is simply highlighting differences and similarities of how the social, economic and environmental domains have been constructed historically and the potential to reconstruct the domains for advancing business, governance and communities. The importance of social contexts, social structures and factors in the theory and practice of CSR and sustainability became relevant within the unit of analyses to address potential pretense in social responsibility. A more accurate representation of social responsibility could be accomplished through greater investigation of society's role and construction of CSR and sustainability since the local community plays a key role in advancing local, regional, and national competitiveness.

Current CSR and sustainability constructs value knowledge as reporting business outcomes in local communities without local community outcomes in business. "There is no direct access to reality unmediated by language and preconceptions" (Astley, 1985: p. 498). McNamee suggests that "locally determined rationalities must also be coordinated with other locally determined rationalities" in a "constant process of discursive engagement that constructs our sense of ethics, truth and knowledge" (1994: p. 72). This study did not assume "problems can be solved with the correct method" (McNamee, 1996: p. 5). Instead, further research addresses the potential for alternative meanings, possibilities and immediate risks of society's preference for business accountability without similar standards of social responsibility for local community accountability. Thus, "there is no truth for all but instead truth within community" (Gergen and Gergen, 2008: p. 71).

CHAPTER 5

Social Domain Strategies

This chapter will discuss recommendations, and potential outcomes within the social domain "for changing competitive pressures and the need for nonmarket strategies" (Doh, Lawton, Rajwani and Paroutis, 2014: p. 96) of corporations and governments working with local communities in CSR and sustainability initiatives and projects. Social domain strategies of well-known corporations are discussed for business, governance and societal relevance, competitiveness and problem formulation in a global volatile economy. In addition, five recommendations and potential outcomes for governments and corporations are discussed with examination of societal competitiveness beyond economic, technological and societal well-being, positive and negative effects of social cohesion and differing local community mindsets for local, regional, national and global competitive advantage with suggestions for advancing the social domain in CSR and sustainability.

Recommendations

Five recommendations were developed from the qualitative and quantitative data results. The recommendations are primarily suitable for socially responsible investors and practitioners in corporations and governments to analyze and develop risk, return and impact (Social Impact Investment Taskforce, 2014a) of social, environmental and economic performance and to influence reputational advantage in CSR and sustainability. Overall, the recommendations are also applicable to any organization involved in CSR, sustainability and development with local communities, governments and corporations. The five recommendations are:

1. Social responsibility approaches from several selected companies be compared and contrasted for potential risk outcomes and indicators.
2. Corporations and governments re-examine formal partnerships and relationships for informal social networks' impacts in products and services.

3. Corporations include the formal and informal society for positive and negative impacts to current CSR and sustainability strategies and competitiveness within financial and non-financial data.
4. Corporations examine social relations in local communities through transdisciplinary methods.
5. Corporations investigate individual drivers in CSR and sustainability social domain strategies for reputational and social risk.

RECOMMENDATION ONE

The social domain strategies of eight selected companies are briefly discussed in recommendation 1 for comparison and contrast of differing business approaches in social responsibility (Table 5.1).

Current CSR and sustainability social strategies from some companies focus on affecting positive social responsibility change with the things that are within the company's control such as supply chain and operations to assure consumers that they are buying products from a responsible company. Other companies strive to decrease social fragmentation through engagement with local communities to fully understand their expectations of a company, employer and community partners, so that the company can identify programs and investments that strengthen their relationships with local communities and give back to the communities where the company's employees live, work and do business.

Recent CSR and sustainability reports from BASF (2012), Campbell Soup (2012), BP (2012), and Ingredion (2012) indicate a focus on corporate philanthropy and CSR and sustainability business strategies to help customers and stakeholders to become more socially responsible. Procter & Gamble utilizes corporate philanthropy and CSR and sustainability business strategies to improve lives and ensure socially responsible operations and services (2012). DuPont focuses on driving sustainability business strategies with introductions of the company's products to help the customer or consumer reduce their impacts with corporate philanthropy complementing DuPont's sustainability business strategies, while CISCO seeks to use its expertise, technology and resources to make a positive contribution to society (DuPont, 2012; CISCO, 2012). Connecting the unconnected and working with others to build thriving communities, improve people's lives and support the long-term success of CISCO's business. To make a significant and lasting impact, CISCO invests in scalable, self-sustaining programs in the areas where CISCO can add the most value.

TABLE 5.1   CURRENT SOCIAL DOMAIN STRATEGIES AND RISK INDICATORS OF SELECTED CORPORATIONS

Company	Social domain strategy	Risk indicators
BP	Local content development strategies Local stakeholder engagement and well-being strategies Corporate philanthropy	Social fragmentation Trust / reputation management Social responsibility / sustainability Knowledge fragmentation
Campbell Soup	Corporate philanthropy Health and wellness of consumers and local communities	Social responsibility / sustainability Knowledge fragmentation
Ingredion	Corporate philanthropy Promoting safety and health Customer collaboration strategies	Social responsibility / sustainability Knowledge fragmentation
BASF	Engage in dialogue with relevant stakeholders Education and international projects	Social responsibility / sustainability Knowledge fragmentation
CISCO	Collaboration through social networks to multiply individual efforts to transform lives, communities and the planet	Social fragmentation Individual driven
Olmix	Collaboration with farmers and large agricultural companies to promote public health and wellness	Social responsibility / sustainability Knowledge fragmentation
DuPont	Protecting people and keeping the environment safe from harm Global presence with each facility leader empowered to work with local community leaders for corporate philanthropy	Social responsibility / sustainability Knowledge fragmentation
Procter & Gamble	Improve and save children's lives, Socially responsible products and services and corporate philanthropy	Social responsibility / sustainability Knowledge fragmentation

CISCO improves access to healthcare, promoting skills development and entrepreneurship, supporting programs that use technology to improve education outcomes and helping non-profit organizations deliver food, clean water, shelter and disaster relief. Likewise, the core business strategy of Olmix services and products are strongly focused on improving animal and human health and wellness, thereby decreasing social responsibility and sustainability knowledge fragmentation with farmers in local communities. Although Olmix, a small–medium enterprise does not currently have the resources for global CSR and sustainability reporting and philanthropy, the company is leading efforts in small–medium enterprise sustainable development goals to create value in business and in the local agricultural communities worldwide (Olmix, n.d.). However, without reciprocation from local communities or stakeholders, social responsibility cannot be sustained solely by corporate philanthropy and business strategies. Consequently, social responsibility/sustainability knowledge fragmentation is the primary risk indicator/outcome.

RECOMMENDATION TWO

Many companies and governments are utilizing social technologies to determine market conditions, being proactive on social issues and working on social relationships. Corporations are dependent upon local communities to achieve successful CSR and sustainability initiatives. For this reason, corporations should evaluate social spatial movement within formal and informal boundaries of a company's customer base. Furthermore, shared and emerging interactions sustain social cohesion. Social progress is a complex undertaking due to individuals' multiple social networks, changing coalitions, hidden agendas and collaboration strategies (Alexander, 1987; Henrich et al., 2001; Stanford, 2001). Therefore, individuals have the capacity to act strategically in social relations at the micro level while managing the macro levels. The formal is supporting the informal society with the informal society playing a stronger role in social motivation and social negotiation that could decrease trust and credibility among corporations, governments and local communities due to individual mobility and migration. Some industries only work with consumers or customers on social platforms and not directly with local communities on the ground. However, local communities are not confined to local areas due to mobility and migration. Therefore, corporations and governments should re-evaluate formal positioning and social cohesion with customers and local communities to evaluate potential limitations with individuals and groups in the informal social networks in local communities beyond surveys due to differing mindsets and varied CSR and sustainability discipline practices of the common good that may not be evident in current products and services.

RECOMMENDATION THREE

Corporations should focus their strategy on how individuals and local communities within formal and informal society can shape and constrain the company's CSR and sustainability strategies and competitiveness within financial and non-financial data. Furthermore, corporations need to be mindful of the changing informal and formal social processes within society that seeks to sustain society's ontological preferences at local, regional, national and global levels. How can companies increase stakeholders' low corporate trust while corporations are dependent upon citizens for competitiveness? Organizational competitiveness is interactional and driven by social relations and institutions at local, regional and national levels (Hakansson, 1982; Storper, 1997). Currently, CSR and sustainability reporting tools depict the social domain as "homoarchy" (Bondarenko, 2005). This requires investigating the intensity, periodicity and duration of relational connections as relationships shift in time, space and cognitive frame (Crumley, 2005) through a transdisciplinary lens. Moreover, culture is not cohesive across geographic localities and situations. Consequently, informal social control systems are liable to promote social deviance and corruption (UNDP, 2004). "Human culture is not just a pool or a source of information; it is an arena and theater of social manipulation and competition via cooperation" (Flinn, 1997: p. 23). Additionally, corporate social performance is to a large extent dependent upon the opinions of others and consists of a "mixture of opinion and ability evaluation" (Festinger, 1954: p. 118). For these reasons, corporations can utilize transdisciplinary research methods (discussed under recommendation four) to improve social performance within the organization's business strategy while enhancing societal progress and knowledge through creating public awareness within an inherent learning process (Lang et al., 2012) for topics such as social performance development, scenario analysis, integrated risk management, differing systems modeling approaches and joint decision-making in partnerships and negotiation (Hadorn et al., 2008). Furthermore, transdisciplinary research can enlarge a narrow range of scenarios that lead to overvaluing the worth and quality, as well as the organizational and strategic choices that can enhance performance (Picone, Dagnino and Mina, 2014). Moreover, competitiveness requires unlearning former successful procedures, operations and successful relationships in a volatile changing global environment. In addition, people and disciplines incorporate an embedded history and evolution that temporarily adapt to current contexts and circumstances but may not be sustainable.

RECOMMENDATION FOUR

Transdisciplinary research focuses on the complexity of perceived connecting case-specific and abstract knowledge from common-good practices and perceptions. Moreover, transdisciplinary research can reveal hidden problems due to a wrong frame of mind or mindset providing understanding of the potential opportunities and limitations with stakeholders to resolve a problem or concern. Likewise, sustainability research challenges the assumptions and practices of established disciplines (Wiek et al., 2012b). Consequently, "problem formulation might be a prolonged social process involving interactions with many individual actors rather than an event involving established formations" (Lang et al., 2012: p. 36). For these reasons, transdisciplinary research can help corporations challenge existing CSR and sustainability practices to enhance innovation and competitive advantage. The social domain is under-developed with a heavy emphasis on socio-economic development, quality of life, well-being, benefits, equality and social satisfaction of people. Moreover, the struggle for the common good, equality and social justice does not take place on a level ontological field. Deutsch argues that "human equality does not imply that people necessarily have the same status, privileges, power, needs, or wealth. It does imply that such differences are not the consequence of one's violation of the other's entitlements" (2006: p. 35). Higher levels of individual responsibility distort social welfare whereas social responsibility can prevent initiative and motivation (Garelli, 1997). Moreover, society is not always hierarchical within formal and informal institutions. Rather, society oftentimes consist of complex patterns of relations that represent heterarchy (Crumley, 1995) resulting in temporary situations, ranking structures and adaptation.

RECOMMENDATION FIVE

Most corporations work within the formal society and create formal social relationships with group selection bias or the right mindset as mentioned by many participants. Participation requires individuals to reflect and adopt a different mindset to distinguish the borders surrounding a problem. Corporations should evaluate how differing local communities' mindsets may constrain formal borders of social responsibility with corporations. Furthermore, the fact of executing things together does not mean that you share the identical right mindset. Without examination of the informal society, the embeddedness of formal social responsibility within CSR and sustainability efforts and strategies can remain detached. Moreover, social and personal responsibility may appear truistic and it is much more complex than what is generally understood and is often practiced as normative conformity in society. For example, social responsibility can also be driven by social approval (Tornatzky and Klein, 1982).

TABLE 5.2   LOCAL COMMUNITY RISK INDICATORS

Quantitative indicator	Risk indicators	Qualitative indicator	Risk indicators
What is the extent and with what frequency / participation did the inputs / contributions of individuals and groups in local communities pursue social responsibility as social service, government dependent, individual or social progress (beyond socio-economic progress) with corporations? What is the frequency and variance over time of positive and negative impacts of local communities on local, regional, national and global competitiveness?	*Local community mindset social service oriented:* may decrease / limit corporate CSR / sustainability capacity in local community *Local community mindset social progress / advancement oriented:* may increase corporate capacity for CSR / sustainability in local community *Local community mindset government oriented:* may decrease / limit corporate CSR / sustainability capacity in local community *Local community mindset individual oriented:* may increase or decrease / limit corporate CSR / sustainability capacity in local community	What are the perceptions (ranking and satisfaction) of individuals and groups in local communities for social responsibility and sustainability without corporate support / partnerships? How do individuals and groups in local communities describe / interpret the formal and informal social processes of CSR / sustainability for innovating products and services?	Social fragmentation Cultural fragmentation Social responsibility / sustainability knowledge fragmentation Individually driven Government dependent Trust / reputation management Local community competitiveness benchmarking

Furthermore, interpretation of positive relationships is socially constructed and can be misleading because the formal positive relationships are not challenging the key individual differences that may exist within informal relationships and support formal positive relationships. A common phrase in society is "they cannot all be like that." However, it takes only one person to change the world or make a difference. Therefore, corporations should evaluate how individual drivers in local communities impact CSR and sustainability and not focus solely on collective behaviors to determine possible fragmented reputational and social risk. Table 5.2 lists potential local community risk indicators for corporations and governments to utilize in current social responsibility strategies within the social domain of CSR and sustainability.

The table includes examples of qualitative and quantitative questions with examples of local mindsets and risk indicators. The risk indicators provide further enhancement and evaluation of social responsibility with customers, local communities and other stakeholders for potential social risk originating from social fragmentation, cultural fragmentation, individual driven, government dependent, trust and reputation management and local community competitiveness benchmarking. Moreover, the qualitative and quantitative indicators and risk indicators provide ways for companies to enhance their portfolios with local communities and reciprocate accountability of CSR and sustainability initiatives back to local communities. Although the indicators in Table 5.2 do not encompass an entire situation and are contextual, they are beneficial to determine local community anti-competitive behavior, lower levels of societal competitiveness in contrast to business competitiveness, and to measure change over time within social processes for benchmarking corporate capacity limitations and outcomes of CSR and sustainability in local communities.

Corporate and Government Potential Outcomes

Most people desire to be helped or served in times of need and in poverty. However, society in formal and informal ways creates social responsibility which influences individuals, groups and organizations on how to deliver social responsibility. Herein lies the challenge. Society has placed more accountability in formal institutions, partnerships, relationships and constructs that result in inconsistent, inadequate and unequal outcomes of social responsibility. Thus, social responsibility pretense is a result of society's social construction of social responsibility. Potential corporate and government outcomes were developed from the recommendations and risk indicators/outcomes in Table 5.2. These outcomes provide corporations and governments across sectors and industries with suggestions to improve and reduce non-intentional pretense of social responsibility strategies within the three domains of CSR and sustainability.

POTENTIAL CORPORATE OUTCOMES

- Greater CSR intelligence and societal strategy of the informal sociological systems and processes and outcomes that direct formal societal movement and impact on financial returns.
- New interpretations of CSR and sustainable development in local communities for innovative products and services.

- Enhanced corporate awareness of the common good in society and business opportunities to change fragmented and conflicting views of how society thinks about the common good through corporate products and services.
- Acknowledging and benchmarking recursive mutual and intermittent societal responsibility and competitiveness behavior inputs and outcomes and dynamic social processes among corporations, individuals and local communities in volatile local markets.
- Corporations hold society accountable by communicating corporate concerns of varying fragmentation among local communities, governments and corporations in CSR and sustainability reports by creating societal competitiveness and societal responsibility indicators as goals and challenges to work together as two through five-year goals.
- Corporations re-evaluate social risk management and reputational risk management within the formal and informal societal conditions in local communities for individual (key stakeholders) and collective normative and non-conformative behavior for greater market share.
- Corporations examine formal and informal markets locally, regionally and nationally to re-evaluate CSR and sustainability partnerships and collaboration for enhanced reputation management.
- Enhanced corporate social risk learning and strategies concerning customers that cooperate formally through corporate partnerships, collaboration and social media and customers that may not sustain the formal behavior through informal social networks in local communities.
- Corporations evaluate individual drivers and not just collective drivers of social responsibility in products and services for customer education and awareness about increasing the role of the local community.
- Re-evaluate corporate formal boundaries to alter the negative dynamics of informal societies on trust and reputation management.

POTENTIAL GOVERNMENT OUTCOMES

- Governments address differing mindsets in local communities to show benefits and provide incentives to link societal competitiveness with technology, economic development and knowledge competitiveness in local communities.

- Governments should investigate social progress and societal competitiveness impacts beyond economic, technological and societal well-being for links to local, regional and national competitiveness.
- Governments should re-evaluate positive and negative drivers, factors, outcomes of social cohesion in local, regional, national and global competitive advantage.
- Governments must look for irregular cultural conflict within local communities due to disruptive social construction and interactions between individuals at micro, meso and macro levels in the informal society and for connections locally, regionally and nationally.

Transforming Society's Role in Social Responsibility within CSR and Sustainability

TRANSDISCIPLINARY RESEARCH IN THE SOCIAL DOMAIN

Moving the social domain forward in CSR and sustainability requires a transdisciplinary approach due to CSR and sustainability discipline fragmentation. Transdisciplinary research integrates interdisciplinary research within differing disciplines and non-academic participants for more sophisticated approaches such as co-production of knowledge (Pohl, 2008). Thus, a transdisciplinary approach may be considered a form of social reconstruction of CSR and sustainability disciplines integrating multiple instruments and measures of different forms of knowledge, social and organizational, communication and technical integration (Bunders et al., 2010). Therefore, utilizing transdisciplinary methods offers problem-solving for issues that are not perceived as problematic such as lack of social responsibility reciprocation from local communities with corporations and an underdeveloped social domain in CSR and sustainability.

A transdisciplinary process addresses and integrates societal and scientific problems through team-building and problem-framing within social construction or co-creation between societal and scientific actors in discourse for societal and scientific practice (Jahn and Keil, 2006). There are important concerns regarding intersecting and integrating disciplines that affect the quality of the research methodologies and data results (Robinson, 2008) and "transdisciplinary projects are too heterogeneous to answer the question directly" (Pohl, 2008: p. 51). However, transdisciplinary research is needed when knowledge about a societal relevant field is uncertain, when the concrete nature of problems is disputed and when there is a great deal at stake for those concerned by problems and involved in dealing with them (Hadorn et al., 2006). Deutschmann argues that "there are clear indications that the capital form of money is taking on functions of collective self-representation in contemporary world society in a latent way, and thus must be conceived of as a fundamental social phenomenon and not only as an economic one" (2012: p. 20). Why is the context of CSR and sustainability treated as an environmental and economic discipline when it is in reality driven by the social domain? The problem is that we are selecting parts of some disciplines without changing the disciplines to address real problems. For example, many sociological disciplines seek to comprehend and focus solely on how identity promotes preferential individual and group behavior. Thus, "unquestioned assumptions about three underlying concepts—discipline, peer and measurement—continue to cloud the discourse on evaluation" (Klein, 2008: p. S121). These assumptions are inadequate to generate new knowledge and require a transdisciplinary approach.

COMMON GOOD IN THE SOCIAL DOMAIN

The common good is a strong ethical theory and principle in CSR and sustainably that warrants further investigation and research of "how it pays to be sustainable" (Schaltegger and Ludeke-Freund, 2012: p. 2). However, transdisciplinary research defines the common good "as being opposite of private interests" (Hadorn et al., 2006: p. 122). Moreover, the common-good approach requires "joint problem framing" (Lang et al., 2012: p. 33) because it lacks social problem-solving capacities due to its emphasis on consensus and equality, well-being and is restricting social and human development and social, environmental and economic progress. Furthermore, without social progress the common good is another way of serving others with no sustainable reciprocation of societal progress. Therefore, social progress cannot be confined to human, environmental and economic well-being (Saisana and Philippas, 2012).

Similar to social responsibility, the common good may drive society to perceive we are all responsible, yet no one is responsible. In addition, multiculturalism may promote divisions and not social cohesiveness due to competing cultural preferences. Galston asks: "How are we to define the limits of the community within which the principle of commonality applies? Environmentalists argue for a global definition: the consumption of fossil fuels produces externalities that affect the entire human race" (2013: p. 12).

This is a one-sided view of the common good that perpetuates a temporary and not an absolute mutual advantage or win–win. Thus, the common-good theory requires problem formulation in attempting to "reconcile values and preferences," because society, business and governance compete for preferred values and norms (Lang et al., 2012: p. 25). Furthermore, is the reconstruction of a unified sense of belonging to a democratic society, regardless of national or ethnic characteristics (Lechat, 2012) the answer for practicing the common good? This may lead to the common good as isomorphic and promotes a very narrow way of determining how well a society progresses and becomes more responsible. Clearly, the reason and will of the individual plays a critical role in the foundation of social order and cohesion (Luhmann, 1981). Therefore, further research into social deviance within the common good should be examined among local communities, governments and corporations because "social order is co-constructed in a recursive process that reconstructs us as persons, relationships and institutions" (Pearce and Pearce, 2000: p. 421).

Social learning within the common good can lead to understanding and cooperation built upon trust and cohesion. Furthermore, greater contact and interactions are more likely to build social cohesion of the desired behavioral effect (Chartrand and Bargh, 1999). However, particular trust can increase social cohesion spatially while decreasing the common good. Moreover, local culture should not be romanticized as the true culture of any ethnic group due to social and individual mobility. Thus, individual and social mobility within the common good requires examination and further research of "determinants of mobility behavior" for "spatial mobility, socio-spatial mobility and social mobility" (Bergmann and Jahn, 2008: p. 5). Furthermore, understanding that local communities are developed within individuals and groups for sustaining identity, reputation and differences and not commonality requires further research into the underlying processes within the larger societal structural contexts for those who pursue the common good and social learning in CSR and sustainability.

Further research is needed to assess societal progress and development beyond unevenly proportioned incomes, poverty and cultural inequality. In addition, future research can address the potential study limitation of overlapping age groups by asking participants to provide their actual age. Perhaps, the organization of society, and not individual behavior is the primary cause of inequality (Rosanvallon, 2012) as most cultures contain unequal elements (Okin, 1999). Therefore, pursuing equality or equity in corporations while society sustains inequality is a social dilemma that warrants further research. Furthermore, institutions and groups are not randomly assigned.

Consequently, this creates perpetual fragmentation among corporations, governments and local communities. Furthermore, equitable respect and trust in diverse cultures is constrained by civil and human rights in the formal society because in reality the diverse cultures do not hold each other equal in the informal society. Additionally, human rights are individually driven in opposition to the state and society (Donnelly, 1984).

Further examination of situational ethnicity within complex polyethnic systems and variation and ambiguity in objective behavior is required to avoid multiculturalism being practiced as a platitude. Moreover, in a multicultural society people are often made to feel shame or guilt when openly discussing ethnic preferences. Axelrod and Hammond provide "proof of the principle that tag-based discrimination can emerge and be maintained under quite minimal conditions, including the absence of reciprocity and reputation" (2003: pp. 7–8). Similarly, risk is perceived by individuals to support a person's way of life (Douglas, 1978). Thus, multicultural communities can appear cohesive and in reality be conflicted and sustain superficially driven relationships resulting in social cooperative bias instead of the common good. Moreover, ethnic cultures that intentionally do not fit or share similar values result in perpetuating others as without merit. Gilroy (2006) describes racial and ethnic differences as a convivial culture where diverse people mix ordinarily with others. This promotes anti-racism in the formal society while sustaining racism in the informal society. Therefore, in sustainable development, favorable local community socio-cultural conditions are in a constant change of flux and because it may not be immediately evident they can constrain sustainable economic development.

SOCIETAL COMPETITIVENESS IN THE SOCIAL DOMAIN

Competitiveness is generally associated with economic or socio-economic and productivity features and is associated and examined by social features. Social value systems, social motivation and social networks are significant factors in the implementation and success for organizational and local, regional and national competitiveness (Garelli, 1997; Wise, 2014). Societal competitiveness requires further research due to society's potential impact to decrease and constrain local, regional and national competitive advantage. Measuring equality by social norms instead of ethnic and other differing personal norms can be misleading. People will compete and compare each other by income, appearance, knowledge and a wide assortment of other interests, while propitiating the decline of national competitiveness, indicating national identity drives a country's performance and competitiveness.

The data shows a gap between local communities and corporations preventing each other from achieving their goals. As not all local communities represent the same values, norms and interests as corporations, the treatment of competitiveness can be based solely on a corporation and an individual. A competitive environment among local communities, corporations and governments requires the local community's willingness to engage with corporate values. However, oftentimes, a competitive social environment is defined as creating jobs and benefitting society's economic well-being. Winning or win–win partnerships do not imply they are competitive. Rather, it is a short-term snapshot focusing on external comparisons to determine individual and group advantage. Furthermore, cooperation and concurrence may result in omitting contest, understanding, knowledge and skillful judgment. Instead, competition is more than achieving short-term goals; it is about sustaining long-term progress and advancement. For these reasons, further research should re-evaluate social cohesiveness effects on local, regional and national competitive advantage for economic, environmental and social risk management.

Conclusion

This volume set out to investigate how local communities, corporations and governments should identify and manage challenges and gaps of social responsibility in CSR and sustainability, establish greater understanding of the role of society within multiple realities of CSR and sustainability and determine factors that lead to an underdeveloped social domain in CSR and sustainability and the lack of local communities' reciprocation in social responsibility to corporations.

The results have important implications for managers and leaders in local communities, governments, corporations and investors seeking social responsible investments (SRI) and social impact investments (SII). Current social domain constructs in CSR and sustainability limit and contribute towards unbalanced social responsibility among corporations, governments and local communities. Furthermore, lack of social responsibility from local communities impacts local, regional, national and global competitiveness, sustains questionable societal values and expectations and decreases social progress due to a lack of critical social and personal development that is crucial for increasing social responsibility among local communities, governments and corporations.

Competitiveness in CSR and sustainability is relationally driven, thereby requiring greater societal competitiveness and social responsibility from local communities for reciprocation to corporations and governments. Individuals and personal trust play a greater role in CSR and sustainability than collaborative partnerships, with local communities dependent upon the government for social responsibility and competitiveness, leaving a gap between corporations and local communities. Trust among individuals, local communities and governments are greater than corporate trust. In the social responsibility model, society is equitable in institutional formal forms, but not within informal forms, because this is something most corporations and governments do not capture. And, it is the informal society that drives social responsibility and competitiveness.

Recommendations and potential outcomes provide corporations with revised social risk indicators and societal strategies for determining formal and informal societal direction on economic and natural environmental returns and transdisciplinary approaches for discipline fragmentation and problem formulation for challenging local communities to reciprocate social responsibility with corporations in a global volatile economy. In addition, recommendations and potential outcomes for governments and corporations include examination of societal competitiveness beyond economic, technological and societal well-being, positive and negative effects of social cohesion and differing local community mindsets for local, regional, national and global competitive advantage. Lastly, suggestions to advance the social domain in CSR and sustainability include transdisciplinary research for discipline fragmentation and "problem formulation" (Lang et al., 2012); the common good for competing cultural preferences and social environments among local communities, governments and corporations; and societal competitiveness to determine society's potential impact on local, regional, national and global competitive advantage in CSR and sustainability.

Appendix

No.	Sustainability	CSR	Definition of social	Trust by group	Other comments	Competitiveness	Values and beliefs by group	Demographics
1	To sustain what we achieved. If poverty eradication is done by supply of food grains. How we are going to meet the continuous supply of food to sustain the eradication of poverty	Corporations never want to be socially responsible. But the public policies of different counties make them or rather held them responsible. Sustainability of corporate responsibility? … I think you will have to find some collation strategies of corporations to have sustainability				Competitiveness as the word itself is confusing in the context of sustainability and SCR … need clarification	Ethical values utilitarian theory and Kant	Asian Kerala, India senior management doctorate male 30–45
2	Meeting today's needs without compromising future			Much needed in all walks of life. Trust deficit create many problems among us		It is the need of hour, makes people more accountable and agile		Indian Kerala, India management graduate male 18–29
3	Sustainability is the ability of improving up on the present situation through continual improvement	CSR has become a very important component in the modern day business and in Indian context also the same is getting more and more important	Social is a broad term which denotes the involvement of people with the society	Trust is something which is based on the internal relationship between the people		Competitiveness is good till the point it benefits the country's economy and the welfare of the people		Asian Kerala, India management doctorate male 18–29
4	Maintaining a process or action once started	Only a few take up any social responsibility		Too old to trust everybody and everything		Competitiveness comes with a dedicated management	Life is God's gift to share	management graduate male 45–60
5	Capacity to accommodate, to adjust with situations							Dravidian management doctorate male 45–60

No.	Definition				Demographics
6	Something that exists for a long period of time				female management doctorate
7	Humans and nature should get along and have harmony	It's very important to have an ethic for everything because the world simply cannot continue consuming at a rising rate while resources begin to fall	In this globalized world where survival of the fittest is the rule, competitiveness is very important	There are many different kind of sense of value between developed countries and emerging countries	Asian West Japan management male 30–45
8	Sustain what you attained			Not related to social corporate responsibility	Asian Kerala India senior management male 30–45
9	Development that meets the needs of the present generation without compromising the ability of the future generations to meet their own needs				management doctorate female 18–29

No.	Sustainability	CSR	Definition of social	Trust by group	Other comments	Competitiveness	Values and beliefs by group	Demographics
10	Strategies that enhance economic, environmental and social performance together	Every effort in the right direction counts	Community			Competitiveness of any entity relies on competitiveness of stakeholders but citizens and communities can get left behind		Washington DC, USA management graduate female 45–60
11	Sustainability is a term used to describe public and private actions that lead to more efficient use of resources. It's a nearly useless term because of the way it has been politicized especially by the right	These terms sustainability, corporate responsibility and corporate social performance—are not the right terms to truly marshal change in communities, regions, and nations	Interconnections between people	Church is defined as a congregation, regardless of religious identification?			Question 47 is false—need government policies to see that economic and environment go together	Caucasian East Coast, USA management doctorate male 45–60
12	Sustainability to me means stewardship and management of resources to enhance productivity to the benefit of the environment							Caucasian Virginia, USA non-management doctorate male 45–60
13	Production, preservation and profit working together		Interacting with others					Caucasian Maryland, USA management graduate male 45–60

#						
14	Socially, economically and environmentally sustainable. Has a reasonable chance of long-term survival	Determining metrics that offers a common platform to compare is needed. Businesses must still remain economically viable and yet demonstrate clear environmental and social standards	Dealing with the welfare of men, women and children, including those with disabilities and different economic classes	There is a gender issue missing here—I have had many co-workers, local businesses and others take advantage of women—therefore I have lost trust	Part of global competitiveness is competing with other countries that have lower environmental and social standards and costs	Caucasian Virginia, USA management undergraduate female 45–60
15	To meet the needs of the present without depleting the regenerative capacity of natural systems to the extent that they are no longer able to sufficiently provide for present and future needs, both human and non-human	True CSR exists in rare instances where the corporate leadership is truly committed / morally compelled, otherwise, there is much green washing and corporate branding about. It is the individual responsibility of shareholders and consumers to hold large corporations accountable	Having to do with interpersonal relations and individual welfare		Hard work can bring a better life however luck and connections are vital for self embitterment	Caucasian Mid-Atlantic, USA non-management graduate male 30–45
16	The use of harvesting which prevents depletion or permanent damage	I am not sure what social responsibility means	Involved with community or outside party			Caucasian Pennsylvania, USA management undergraduate male 45–60

No.	Sustainability	CSR	Definition of social	Trust by group	Other comments	Competitiveness	Values and beliefs by group	Demographics
17	An integrated system of production practices to satisfy human food and fiber needs that is socially acceptable, environmentally sound and economically viable	My response to stated questions is limited to my knowledge / experience focused on US agricultural production sector only		For Question 34 need more levels for response than three as indicated				Asian–American Washington DC, USA, management doctorate male 45–60
18	Bruntland definition mixed with Elkington definition of the TBL		Benefitting the human condition					Caucasian–European San Francisco, USA management graduate female 30–44
19	The ability of future generations of people to have the same opportunity and access to a clean, healthy environment; personal health; and economic opportunity		Having to do with other people					Caucasian Washington, DC, USA non-management graduate female 30–45
20	Sustainability is the interaction of responsibility between people their environment, economics, and social interactions under a long-term timeline		Interacting with other people					Caucasian Takoma Park, MD, USA senior management graduate male 60–75

#			
21	Continuous renewal of resources and materials for continuation of humanity, focus not really on environmental continuity for its own sake			Incomplete 161.80.112.162
22	Prudently managing natural resources today with a perspective of keeping in mind the same resources for future generations			Caucasian Washington, DC, USA graduate male 45–60
23	Future Generations	Generally, the perception is that sustainability relates to environmental impacts. There is a need to get away from the term "social responsibility" and more towards sustainability	Competitiveness occurs when people perceive themselves to have self-efficacy and that must start at the individual	Caucasian Arkansas, USA management doctorate female 30–45
24	3 pillar equity	The noun, verb or adjective? I'm assuming you mean the public good?		Caucasian USA non-management graduate female 45–60

No.	Sustainability	CSR	Definition of social	Trust by group	Other comments	Competitiveness	Values and beliefs by group	Demographics
25	Future Generations		Relating to society	People would probably take advantage of you				Caucasian Virginia, USA non-management female 30–45
26	3 pillar long term		Human Rights					Caucasian Iowa, USA management graduate female 30–45
27	Business Does not harm quality of life or environment		Benefitt ng society					White Virginia, USA non-management graduate female 30–45
28	Brundlandt							Incomplete 212.137.36.236
29	Meeting my needs without impacting others doing the same							Incomplete 161.80.24.51
30	Long-term issues	All three required for long-term global population	All interactions with others	Contextual		Corporations, citizens, government at all levels must work together successfully		American Virginia, USA management undergraduate male 45–60

No.	Statement		Response	Notes		Comment	Demographics
31	System that will not deplete resources or harm natural cycles	Companies appear to be acting more socially responsible until the media unearths information about their bad practices—like bribing other countries to get out around regulations. Makes it difficult to have a lot of faith in what companies preach (e.g., Walmart)		Not applicable. Should apply to some of the questions above such as people of another religion or nationality, as that does not impact my trust in people			White Washington, DC, USA management graduate female 30–45
32	Brundlandt		Doing right for the people				White Arizona, USA senior management undergraduate male 30–45
33	Brundlandt		Interpersonal, institutions and human interactions			Definition problem—difficult to answer	White West Coast, USA senior management doctorate female 45–60
34	3 pillars over time		Interaction with other people				American East Coast, USA non-management doctorate male 60–75

No.	Sustainability	CSR	Definition of social	Trust by group	Other comments	Competitiveness	Values and beliefs by group	Demographics
35	SD overtime and 3 pillar prosperity		Interaction with people					White, non-management doctorate female 60–75
36	Brundlandt							White Virginia, USA non-management graduate male 45–60
37	Future generations							Latino, West Coast, USA management graduate female 45–60
38	3 pillars based upon international secondary sources	Business imperative						Incomplete 194.113.59.80

#	Response						Demographics
39	I think of sustainability as a balance between people, profit and planet (triple bottom line). To live sustainably, we must not deplete or degrade our natural resources or ecosystems, we must consider the quality of life of all people, yet we must balance these two elements with the ability to progress and develop as a society	Giving companies a platform locally, regionally and globally					Incomplete 204.74.20.14
40	Lasting products—environmentally friendly and energy efficient						White USA non-management undergraduate female 30–45
41	Brundlandt						White Nebraska, USA senior management graduate female 45–60

No.	Sustainability	CSR	Definition of social	Trust by group	Other comments	Competitiveness	Values and beliefs by group	Demographics
42	To borrow from Gifford Pichot: "Sustainability is the application of common sense to the common problems for the common good"	To borrow once again from Pichot: "Sustainability is the foresighted utilization, preservation and/ or renewal of forests, waters, lands and minerals, for the greatest good of the greatest number for the longest time"	Our orientation and interaction with others, the process of creating allies	Pichot again: "The earth and its resources belong of right to its people"				White, Washington, DC, USA senior management graduate male 45–60
43	3 pillar long-term		Service to society to insure well being of people					French Brittany France management doctorate female 18–29
44	Evolution without destruction	There is no other way to evolve as human beings in a "commercial world"	me vs others vs me	I trust in my family and in God. All the rest is relative		Question marks for question 26 with no answer—we should do better, not necessary more. growing faster than world is not the way	Question 40—God said to work and make money by wealding—only delinquents work without effort including speculators	Navara, Spain senior management college male 45–60
45	3 pillar long-term	I believe that only the person and company who will get a good balance between all this point will have good and prosperous time	Take care of people around us					French Brittany, France management graduate male 18–29

#		Relationships between people			
46	Way to have a lasting activity balancing environmental, social and economical concerns				French Brittany France non-management doctorate female 18–29
47	Brief life or short-term action	Regarding people of another religion or nationality, it just depends on "Do I know them personally or not?" No difference according to nationality or religion			French Brittany, France management college male 30–45
48	No response				French female
49	Consideration of social and environmental aspects in the development strategy of the company				European Brittany, France management graduate female 30–45
50	Consideration of environmental aspects in the development strategy of the company				European Brittany, France management graduate female 30–45
51	Efficient use of energy and responsible policy on waste disposal	Interrelation with friends, family, co-workers, community			Black–Latino management graduate female 45–60

No.	Sustainability	CSR	Definition of social	Trust by group	Other comments	Competitiveness	Values and beliefs by group	Demographics
52	Brundlandt							French Ho Chi Minh City, Vietnam management graduate male 45–60
53	Long-term growth				High performance			Vietnamese Ho Chi Minh City, Vietnam management doctorate male 30–45
54	Long-term growth	Do not know what it is						Latino, North Holland, Netherlands non-management graduate female 30–45
55	Brundlandt	Accountability is critical to creating a truly equitable and balanced society	That we are thinking about "social." the word relates to [sic]					Colorado, USA non-management graduate male 60–75
56	The capacity to endure							France management graduate male 18–29M
57	Independence							not completed

#					
58	Sustainability is: Create value and livings without damage to the earth and human beings	The company I work for has for purpose to develop natural solution in a sustainable way, green chemistry for animal husbandry and crop rising. It is today essential to produce food in quantities to feed 9 billion people in 2050 but this has to be done in the respect of animals and nature. The range we develop is made for welfare, hygiene and efficiency of animal nutrition, using less antibiotics and chemicals such as pesticide. Working for this company, I have the feeling to work in a sustainable spirit. It was part of the reason I wanted to work for it. We also work daily with people from all religion, all countries, all languages, learning more about different culture. This is part of our mission	Trust is not easy to give right from the beginning. I have the great chance to be helped by people that had more trust and gave it to me from first seeing. Come back in few years and there will be more X on the left	Competitiveness is not being put against social responsibility but with it. It is very important that we can grow an enterprise the good way as long as the people giving the effort see the payback. This is to me the important part that we can see in a family enterprise like the one I work for. Also the money earn by the company is put back into it R&D investment and better work condition. This gives more competitiveness but at the company level	French Brittany France management graduate male 30-45
59	Development based on a balance societal, economical and environmental				French Brittany, France management graduate male

No.	Sustainability	CSR	Definition of social	Trust by group	Other comments	Competitiveness	Values and beliefs by group	Demographics
60	Preserve our resources and used to better	Too social not only empowers people		Trust earned over time and achieves	Competitiveness depends not only businesses but also the policies put in place by the authorities		Work always pays at one time or another and requires relations with others	French Senegal, Africa non-management undergraduate male 30–45
61	Consideration of environmental and social concepts on a global scale, government and business							European Brittany, France non-management graduate female 18–29
62	Economic development that respects the environment and social rights							Port Louis, France management graduate female 30–45
63	Economic growth	Social crisis facing the sustainable development and social responsibility are very important			Responsible society			Brittany, France senior management doctorate female 30–45

64	Adaptation and assimilation complete integrated solutions and effective long term and continually involving responsibility towards the generations to come, creating a culture and style of living in accordance with the present and future resources	These concepts are radically transforming the lives and sense of human beings and that existing systems are still theories and discourses in vogue for us and our governments, but they are aware and reconsider our attitude towards ourselves and our planet, by understanding and assimilating first-level staff at each level and after the community ... nations to become reality, and put into practice	A positive, constructive and responsible in continuing the good things our predecessors, we solidarizing to recreate on a solid foundation of our society	Question 17—They [CSR, Sustainability and CSP] determine the competitiveness	Continuously cultivate the relational levels of life and true educational values that surround us	Romanian Giurigu, Romania management graduate female 30–45
65	Efforts address triple bottom line—social, environmental, and economic viability		Combination of what comes out of investigative journalism and science fiction			White USA management graduate female 18–29
66	Choose the means of development (especially industrial) today in a way that will not affect the life and development of tomorrow					Romanian Bucharest, Romania non-management doctorate male 45–60

No.	Sustainability	CSR	Definition of social	Trust by group	Other comments	Competitiveness	Values and beliefs by group	Demographics
67	The process of continued use of a resource or system with continued effectiveness of the outcome		Involving others					management doctorate male 45–60
68	Systems must be sustainable environmentally, economically and socially							White Fredericksburg, VA, USA management doctorate male 45–60
69	Processes where there is no environmental degradation and where the natural resources being consumed are completely renewable							White Maryland, USA management doctorate male 60–75
70	3 pillar							Mid-Atlantic, USA management doctorate male 45–60

No.						Demographics
71	Balancing agricultural, industrial and intellectual productivity with the conservation, preservation and restoration of the earth's natural resources for future generations	Can companies practice CSR without bothering with sustainability as I defined it? I believe they can	Trust is earned		How does the individual fit in, when most of the CSR and competitiveness evaluations are at the macro level?	White Mid-Atlantic, USA senior management doctorate male 45–60
72	How we operate in the social, cultural, and economic environment within the context of our work					White Mid-Atlantic, USA senior management graduate female 45–60
73	Long term productive, economic, environmental and social viability					White USA management graduate male 45–60
74	Sustainability is the possibility to pass the world on to our children					French Upper Normandy, France management graduate female 18–29

No.	Sustainability	CSR	Definition of social	Trust by group	Other comments	Competitiveness	Values and beliefs by group	Demographics
75	Decision making that considers the three pillars simultaneously							White Nebraska, USA management graduate male 60-75
76	Brundlandt and 3 pillars							Beijing, China senior management graduate male 18-29
77	Long-term 3 pillars environment = (social and nature)	Good balance = good progress over time	Take care of people around us					French Brittany, France management graduate male
78	Sustainability is the principle or term used to describe conditions or atmosphere created to ensure that an activity, or plan can be viable for present situations and also for long term effects without compromising itself or the factor involved	It can be merged together for the good of society		Trust completely makes it difficult to choose unless. In my case, my mum and siblings. I would choose trust completely. However, family there is too big for me				Greater Accra, Ghana non-management undergraduate male 18-29

#					
79	Using fewer resources for well human deeds with reducing its impact in environment and on the local people	Each and every person of the society is responsible for their environment and to live in a good situation with all their sources they have BUT with less environmental impacts. The people should understand these three points and to be socially responsible. But there has to be someone to transfer these messages to the local people who have not heard about corporate social responsibility	In each and every step of life trust is important to keep relationship and develop our business	Serve others in the community	Afghan Afghanistan management doctorate male 18–29
80	Cf King of Thailand and Sustainable development				Indonesia non-management doctorate male 18–29
81	something that can stand a long time	The way of life of people			management doctorate male 40–45

References

Adams, C. and Zutshi, A. (2004). Corporate Social Responsibility: Why Business Should Act Responsibly and Be Accountable. *Australian Accounting Review*, 14(3), 31–9.

Agenda 21 (2012). *Rio + 20: Sustainable Development Goals (SDGs)*. Available at: www.uncsd2012.org/content/documents/colombiasdgs.pdf (accessed 10 September 2012).

Aguilera, R.V., Rupp, D.E., Williams, C.A. and Ganapathi, J. (2007). Putting the S Back in Corporate Social Responsibility: A Multilevel Theory of Social Change in Organizations. *Academy of Management Review*, 32(3), 836–63.

Alexander, R.D. (1987). *The Biology of Moral Systems*. Hawthorne, NY: Aldine de Gruyter.

Alkhafaji, A.F. (1989). *A Stakeholder Approach to Corporate Governance: Managing in a Dynamic Environment*. New York: Quorum Books.

Alon, I., Lattemann, C., Fetscherin, M., Li, S. and Schneider, A.M. (2010). Usage of Public Corporate Communications of Social Responsibility in Brazil, Russia, India and China (BRIC). *International Journal of Emerging Markets*, 5(1), 6–22.

Alperovitz, A., Dubb, S. and Howard, T. (2007). *7 Cool Companies*. Available at: www.yesmagazine.org (accessed 8 October 2014).

Amaeshi, K.M., Osuji, O. and Nnodim, P. (2008). Corporate Social Responsibility in Supply Chains of Global Brands: A Boundaryless Responsibility? Clarification, Exceptions and Implications. *Journal of Business Ethics*, 81(1), 223–34.

——, Ezeoha, A.E., Adi, B.C. and Nwafor, M. (2007). *Financial Exclusion and Strategic Corporate Social Responsibility: A Missing Link in Sustainable Finance Discourse?* No. 49-2007 ICCSR Research Paper Series—ISSN 1479-5124. Available at: http://www.nottingham.ac.uk/business/ICCSR (accessed 2 September 2009).

Anderson, J.W. (1989). *Corporate Social Responsibility.* Westport, CT: Greenwood Press.

Arnstein, S.R. (1969). A Ladder of Citizen Participation. *Journal of the American Institute of Planners*, 35(4), 216–24.

Aslaender, M.S. and Curbach, J. (2015). Corporate Governmental Duties? Corporate Citizenship From a Governmental Perspective. *Business and Society*, DOI: 10.1177/0007650315585974, 1–9.

Astley, W.G. (1985). Administrative Science as Socially Constructed Truth. *Administrative Science Quarterly*, 30(4), 497–513.

Avi-Yonah, R. (2006). *Corporate Social Responsibility and Strategic Tax Behavior.* University of Michigan Program in Law and Economics Archive: 2003–2009. Working Paper 65.

Axelrod, R. (1984). *The Evolution of Cooperation.* New York: Basic Books.

—— and Hammond, R.A. (2003). The Evolution of Ethnocentric Behavior. *Journal of Conflict Resolution*, 50(6), 926–36.

Banerjee, S.B. (2001). Corporate Social Responsibility: The Good, the Bad and the Ugly. *Critical Sociology*, 34(1), 51–79.

Bansal, P. and Roth, K. (2000). Why Companies Go Green: A Model of Ecological Responsiveness. *Academy of Management Journal*, 43, 717–36.

——, Gao, J. and Qureshi, I. (2014). The Extensiveness of Corporate Social and Environmental Commitment across Firms over Time. *Organizational Studies*, 35(97), 949–66.

Barnett, M.L. (2007). Stakeholder Influence Capacity and the Variability of Financial Returns to Corporate Social Responsibility. *Academy of Management Review*, 32(3), 794–816.

BASF (2012). *Report*. Available at: www.basf.com (accessed 1 March 2013).

Batie, S.S. (1989). Sustainable Development: Challenges to the Profession of Agricultural Economics. *American Journal of Agricultural Economics*, 71(5), 1083–101.

Baumgartner, S. and Quaas, M. (2010). What is Sustainability Economics? *Ecological Economics*, 69, 445–50.

Bečić, E., Mulej, E.M. and Švarc, J. (2012). Measuring Social Progress by Sustainable Development Indicators: Cases of Croatia and Slovenia. *Social and Behavioral Sciences*, 37, 458–65.

Benabou, R. and Tirole, J. (2010). *Individual and Corporate Social Responsibility*. Institutions and Markets Series, Fondazione Eni Enrico Mattei. Available at: www.feem.it (accessed 12 January 2013).

Bergmann, M. and Jahn, T. (2008). CITY: Mobil: A Model for Integration in Sustainability Research. In Hadorn, G.H., Hoffman-Reim, H., Biber-Klemm, S., Grossenbacher-Mansuy, W., Joye, D., Pohl, C., Wiesmann, U. and Zemp, E. (eds), *Handbook of Transdisciplinary Research*. Basel: Springer.

Berman, S.L., Wicks, A.C., Kotha, S. and Jones, T.M. (1999). Does Stakeholder Orientation Matter? The Relationship between Stakeholder Management Models and Firm Financial Performance. *Academy of Management Journal*, 42(5), 488–506.

Bhattacharya, C.B. and Sen, S. (2003). Consumer–Company Identification: A Framework for Understanding Consumers' Relationships with Companies. *Journal of Marketing*, 67(2), 76–88.

Blindheim, B.T. (2011). *Institutional Convergent Alternatives to Instrumental and Ethical Corporate Social Responsibility Perspectives*. Presentation given at the 17th Annual Conference of the International Sustainable Development Society (ISDRS). Columbia University, New York, 9 May 2011.

—— and Mikkelsen, A. (2008). Corporate Social Responsibility. In Mikkelsen, A. and Langhelle, O. (eds), *Arctic Oil and Gas: Sustainability at Risk*. London: Routledge.

Bondarenko, D.M. (2005). A Homoarchic Alternative to the Homoarchic State: Benin Kingdom of the 13th–19th Centuries. *Social Evolution and History*, 4(2), 18–88.

Bossel, H. (2000). The Human Actor in Ecological–Economic Models: Policy Assessment and Simulation of Actor Orientation for Sustainable Development. *Ecological Economics*, 34, 337–55.

Bowen, H.R. (1953). *Social Responsibilities of the Businessman*. New York: Harper and Row.

BP (2012). *Building a Stronger, Safer BP: Sustainability Review Report*. Available at: www.bp.com (accessed 1 May 2013).

Brammer, S., Jackson, G. and Matten, D. (2012). Corporate Social Responsibility and Institutional Theory: New Perspectives on Private Governance. *Socio-Economic Review*, 10, 3–28.

Branco, M.C. and Rodrigues, L.L. (2006). Corporate Social Responsibility and Resource-Based Perspectives. *Journal of Business Ethics*, 69, 111–32.

Brenner, S. and Cochran, P.L. (1991). The Stakeholder Theory of the Firm: Implications for Business and Society Theory and Research. *Proceedings of the International Association for Business and Society*, 449–67.

Brummer, J. (1991). *Corporate Responsibility and Legitimacy*. New York: Greenwood Press.

Brundiers, K. and Wiek, A. (2010). Educating Students in Real-World Sustainability Research: Vision and Implementation. *Innovative Higher Education*, 36(2), 107–24.

Bunders, J.F.G., Broerse, J.E.W., Keil, F., Pohl, C., Scholz, R.W. and Zweekhorst, B.M. (2010). How Can Transdisciplinary Research Contribute to Knowledge Democracy? In Roeland, J. (ed.), *Knowledge Democracy. Consequences for Science, Politics and Media*. Berlin: Springer, 125–52.

Burchell, J. and Cook, J. (2006). Confronting the Corporate Citizen: Shaping the Discourse of Corporate Social Responsibility. *International Journal of Sociology and Social Policy*, 26(3/4), 121–37.

—— (2008). Stakeholder Dialogue and Organizational Learning: Changing Relationships between Companies and NGOs. *Business Ethics: A European Review*, 17(1), 35–46.

Burns, N. and Grove, S.K. (2005). *The Practice of Nursing Research: Conduct, Critique, and Utilization*, 5th edn. St. Louis: Elsevier Saunders.

Callan, M.J., Kay, A.C., Olson, J.M., Brar, N. and Whitefield, N. (2010). The Effects of Priming Legal Concepts on Perceived Trust and Competitiveness, Self-Interested Attitudes and Competitive Behavior. *Journal of Experimental Social Psychology*, 46, 325–35.

Campbell, K. and Vick, D. (2007). Disclosure Law and the Market for Corporate Social Responsibility. In McBarnet, D., Voiculescu, A. and Campbell, T. (eds), *The New Corporate Accountability: Corporate Social Responsibility and the Law*. Cambridge: Cambridge University Press, 241–78.

Campbell Soup (2012). *Campbell's CSR Report*. Available at: www. campbellsoup.com (accessed 1 March 2013).

Carroll, A.B. (1979). A Three-Dimensional Conceptual Model of Corporate Performance. *Academy of Management Review*, 4(4), 497–505.

—— (1991). The Pyramid of Corporate Social Responsibility: Towards the Moral Management of Organizational Stakeholders. *Business Horizons* (July–August), 39–48.

—— (1999). Corporate Social Responsibility: Evolution of a Definitional Construct. *Business and Society*, 38(3), 1–28.

—— and Shabana, K.M. (2010). The Business Case for Corporate Social Responsibility: A Review of Concepts, Research and Practice. *International Journal of Management Reviews*, 12(1), 85–105.

Carruthers, G. and Tinning, G. (2003). Where, and How, do Monitoring and Sustainability Indicators Fit into Environmental Management Systems? *Australian Journal of Experimental Agriculture*, 43(3), 307–23.

Chartrand, T.L. and Bargh, J.A. (1999). The Chameleon Effect: The Perception–Behavior Link and Social Interaction. *Journal of Personality and Social Psychology*, 76(3), 893–910.

CISCO (2012). CSR Report. Available at: www.CISCO.com (accessed 1 March 2013).

Clarkson, M.B.E. (1991). Defining, Evaluating and Managing Corporate Social Performance: The Stakeholder Management Model. In Post, J.E. (ed.), *Research in Corporate Social Performance and Policy*, vol. 12. Greenwich, CT: JAI Press, 331–58.

—— (1995). A Stakeholder Framework for Analyzing and Evaluating Corporate Social Performance. *Academy of Management Review*, 20, 65–91.

Collins, J.C. and Porras, J.I. (1996). Building Your Company's Vision. *Harvard Business Review*, 74(5), 65–77.

Cooper, S.M. and Owen, D.L. (2007) Corporate Social Reporting and Stakeholder Accountability: The Missing Link. *Accounting, Organizations and Society*, 32, 649–67.

Corbiere-Nicollier, T., Laban, B.G., Lindquist, L., Leterrier, Y., Manson, J.A.E. and Jolliet, O. (2002). Lifecycle Assessment of Biofibers Replacing Glass Fibers as Reinforcement in Plastics. *Resource Conservation Recycling*, 33(4), 267–87.

Costanza, R. and Patten, B.C. (1995). Defining and Predicting Sustainability. *Ecological Economics*, 15, 193–6.

Crumley, C.L. (1995). Heterarchy and the Analysis of Complex Societies. *Archeological Papers of the American Anthropological Association*, 6(1), 1–5.

—— (2005). Remember How to Organize: Heterarchy across Disciplines. In Beekman, C.S. and Baden, W.W. (eds), *Nonlinear Models for Archaeology and Anthropology: Continuing the Revolution.* Aldershot: Ashgate.

Dahlsrud, A. (2008). How Corporate Social Responsibility is Defined: An Analysis of 37 Definitions. *Corporate Social Responsibility and Environmental Management*, 15(1), 1–13.

Daly, H. (1977). *Steady-State Economics.* San Francisco: W.H. Freeman and Co.

Davis, K. (1973). The Case For and Against Business Assumption of Social Responsibilities. *Academy of Management Journal*, 16, 312–22.

De Bakker, G.A., Groenewegen, P. and Den Hond, F. (2005). A Bibliometric Analysis of 30 Years of Research and Theory on Corporate Social Responsibility and Corporate Social Performance. *Business and Society*, 44(3), 283–317.

Dentchev, N. (2004). Corporate Social Performance as a Business Strategy, *Journal of Business Ethics*, 55(4), 397–412.

DePrins, M., Devooght, K., Janssens, G. and Moldcrcz, I. (2009). *Social Responsibility Business: From Strategic Vision to Operational Approach.* Antwerp: De Boeck.

Deutsch, M. (2006). Cooperation and Competition. In Deutsch, M. and Coleman, E.C.M. (eds), *The Handbook of Conflict Resolution: Theory and Practice.* San Francisco: Jossey-Bass, 23–42.

Deutschmann, C. (2012). Capitalism, Religion, and the Idea of the Demonic. *Max-Planck Institute for the Study of Societies, Discussion Paper*, 12(2).

Doh, J.P., Lawton, T.C., Rajwani, T. and Paroutis, S. (2014). Why Your Company May Need a Chief External Officer: Upgrading External Affairs Can Help Align Strategy and Improve Competitive Advantage. *Organizational Dynamics*, 43(2), 94–104.

Donaldson, T. and Preston, L.E. (1995). The Stakeholder Theory of the Corporation: Concepts, Evidence, and Implications. *Academy of Management Review*, 20(1), 65–91.

Donnelly, J. (1984). Cultural Relativism and Universal Human Rights. *Human Rights Quarterly*, 6(4), 400–419.

Douglas, M. (1978). *Cultural Bias*. Royal Anthropological Institute Occasional Paper 35.

Dowd, K. (2014). *Math Gone Mad: Regulatory Risk Modeling by the Federal Reserve*. CATO Institute Policy Analysis Number 754. Available at: www.catoinstitute.org (accessed 5 September 2014).

Du, S., Bhattacharya, C.B. and Sen, S. (2007). Reaping Relational Rewards from Corporate Social Responsibility: The Role of Competitive Positioning. *International Journal of Research in Marketing*, 24, 224–41.

DuPont (2012). Sustainability Progress Report. Available at: www.dupont.com (accessed 1 May 2013).

Durham, W. (1991). *Coevolution: Genes, Culture and Human Diversity*. California: Stanford University Press.

Dutta, P.K., Lach, S. and Rustichini, A. (1995). Better Late than Early: Vertical Differentiation in the Adoption of a New Technology. *Journal of Economics and Management Strategy*, 4, 563–89.

Ekins, P. (1992). *A New World Order: Grassroots Movements for Global Change*. New York: Routledge.

Falck, O. and Heblich, S. (2007). Corporate Social Responsibility: Doing Well by Doing Good. *Business Horizons*, 50(3), 247–54.

Festinger, L. (1954). A Theory of Social Comparison Processes. *Human Relations*, 7, 117–40.

Filatotchev, I. and Nakajima, C. (2014). Corporate Governance, Responsible Managerial Behavior, and Corporate Social Responsibility: Organizational Efficiency versus Organizational Legitimacy? *Academy of Management Perspective*, 28(3), 289–306.

Flinn, M.V. (1997). Culture and the Evolution of Social Learning. *Evolution and Human Behavior*, 18(1), 23–67.

Forrest, R. and Kearns, A. (2001). Social Cohesion, Social Capital and the Neighborhood. *Urban Studies*, 38, 2125–43.

Freeman, R.E. (1984). *Strategic Management: A Stakeholder Perspective.* Englewood Cliffs, NJ: Prentice Hall.

—— (2002). Stakeholder Theory of the Modern Corporation. In Donaldson, T. and Werhane, P. (eds), *Ethical Issues in Business: A Philosophical Approach*, 7th edn. Englewood Cliffs, NJ: Prentice Hall, 38–48.

—— Harrison, J.S. and Wicks, A.C. (2007). *Managing for Stakeholders: Survival, Reputation, and Success.* New Haven, CT: Yale University Press.

Friedman, M. (1970). The Social Responsibility of Business is to Increase its Profits. *New York Times Magazine* (13 September), 32–3, 122, 126.

Gaines, S.E. (2006). Sustainable Development and National Security. *William and Mary Environmental Law and Policy Review*, 30(2), 321–70.

Gale, D. (1996). What Have We Learned from Social Learning? *European Economic Review*, 40, 617–28.

Gallimore, R., Goldenberg, C.N. and Weisner, T.S. (1993). The Social Construction and Subjective Reality of Activity Settings: Implications for Community Psychology. *American Journal of Community Psychology*, 21(4), 537–59.

Galston, W.A. (2013). The Common Good: Theoretical Content, Practical Utility. *Daedalus: The Journal of the American Academy of Arts and Sciences,* 142(2), 9–14.

Garelli, S. (1997). The Four Fundamental Forces of Competiveness. Available at: www.imd.ch/wcy/approach/fundamentals.html (accessed 1 May 2013).

Garriga, E. and Mele, D. (2004). Corporate Social Responsibility Theories: Mapping the Territory. *Journal of Business Ethics,* 53(1/2), 51–71.

Gergen, K.J. (1985). The Social Constructionist Movement in Modern Psychology. *American Psychologist,* 40(3), 266–75.

—— and Gergen, M. (2000). The New Aging: Self Construction and Social Values. In Schaie, K.W. (ed.), *Social Structures and Aging.* New York: Springer.

—— (2008). *Social Construction: Entering the Dialogue.* Chagrin Falls, OH: Taos Institute Publications.

Gilroy, P. (2006). *After Empire: Multicultural or Postcolonial Melancholia.* London: Routledge.

Giovannini, E. (2004). *Progress Measuring Progress.* OECD. First World Forum on Key Indicators Statistics, Knowledge and Policy. Palermo, Italy, November 2004. Available at: www.oecd.org (accessed 9 October 2014).

Gladwin, T.N., Kennelly, J.J. and Krause, T.S. (1995). Shifting Paradigms for Sustainable Development: Implications for Management Theory and Research. *Academy of Management Review,* 20(4), 874–907.

Godfrey, P.C. and Hatch, N.W. (2007). Researching Corporate Social Responsibility: An Agenda for the 21st Century. *Journal of Business Ethics,* 70, 88–95.

Goodpaster, K.E. (1991). Business Ethics and Stakeholder. *Business Ethics Quarterly,* 1, 53–72.

Gond, J.-P. and Crane, A. (2008). Corporate Social Performance Disoriented: Saving the Lost Paradigm? *Business and Society*, 20(10), 2–20.

—— and Matten, D. (2007). *Rethinking the Business-Society Interface: Beyond the Functionalist Trap.* No. 47-2007 ICCSR Research Paper Series — ISSN 1479-5124. Available at: http://www.nottingham.ac.uk/business/ICCSR (accessed 12 September 2009).

—— Kang, N. and Moon, J. (2011). The Government of Self-Regulation: On the Comparative Dynamics of Corporate Social Responsibility. *Economy and Society*, 40(4), 640–71.

Graafland, J.J., Eijffinger, S.C.W. and Smid, H. (2004). Benchmarking of Corporate Social Responsibility: Methodological Problems and Robustness. *Journal of Business Ethics*, 53(1/2), 137–52.

GRI [Global Reporting Initiative] (2014). *G4 Sustainability Reporting Guidelines.* Available at: www.globalreporting.org (accessed 15 September 2014).

Hadorn, G.H., Bradley, D., Pohl, C., Rist, S. and Wiesmann, U. (2006). Implications of Transdisciplinary for Sustainability Research. *Ecological Economics*, 60, 119–28.

——, Hoffman-Reim, H., Biber-Klemm, S., Grossenbacher-Mansuy, W., Joye, D., Pohl, C., Wiesmann, U. and Zemp, E. (eds) (2008). *Handbook of Transdisciplinary Research.* Basel: Springer.

Hakansson, H. (ed.) (1982). *International Marketing and Purchasing of Industrial Goods: A Network Approach.* London: Crom Helm.

Hart, O. (1995). Corporate Governance: Some Theory and Implications. *Economic Journal*, 105(430), 678–89.

Haughton, G. (1999). Environmental Justice and the Sustainable City. *Journal of Planning Education and Research*, 18, 233–43.

Hayek, F.A. (1960). *The Constitution of Liberty.* London: Routledge.

Heald, M. (1970). *The Social Responsibilities of Business: Company and Community, 1900–1960*. Cleveland, OH: Case Western Reserve University Press.

Henrich, J. (2004). Cultural Group Selection, Coevolutionary Processes and Large-Scale Cooperation. *Journal of Economic Behavior and Organization*, 53, 85–8.

——, Boyd, R., Bowles, S., Camerer, C., Fehr, C., Gintis, H. and McElreath, R. (2001). Cooperation, Reciprocity and Punishment in Fifteen Small-Scale Societies. *American Economic Review*, 91, 73–8.

Hill, C.W.L. and Jones, T.N. (1992). Stakeholder-Agency Theory. *Journal of Management Studies*, 29(2), 131–54.

Hogg, M.A. and Reid, S.A. (2006). Social Identity, Self-Categorization, and the Communication of Group Norms. *Communication Theory*, 16, 7–30.

Hoppe, H. and Lehmann-Grube, U. (2001). Second-Mover Advantages in Dynamic Quality Competition. *Journal of Economics and Management Strategy*, 10, 419–33.

Hosseini, J.C. and Brenner, S.N. (1992). The Stakeholder Theory of the Firm. *Business Ethics Quarterly*, 2(2), 99–119.

House, R., Rousseau, D.M. and Thomas-Hunt, M. (1995). The Meso Paradigm: A Framework for the Integration of Micro and Macro Organizational Behavior. In Cummings, L.L. and Staw, B.M. (eds), *Research in Organizational Behavior*, vol. 17. Stamford, CT: JAI Press, 71–114.

Hu, D. (2014). *Corporate Social Responsibility (CSR) Governance into Sustainable Development*. In International Conference on Global Economy, Commerce and Service Science (GECSS 2014). Beijing: Atlantis Press, 225–8.

Huge, J. and Waas, T. (2011). *Corporate Social Responsibility for Sustainable Development: Reflections on Theory, Practice and on the Role of Government*. The Flemish Policy Research Centre for Sustainable Development Working Paper No. 29.

Iamandi, I. (2007). Corporate Social Responsibility and Social Responsiveness in a Global Business Environment: A Comparative Theoretical Approach. *Romanian Economic Journal*, 23(June), 1–18.

Ingredion (2012). *Ingredients of a Sustainable Company 2012 Sustainability Update Report.* Available at: www.ingredion.com (accessed 1 May 2013).

Integrated Reporting (2013). *The Integrated Reporting Framework.* Available at: www.theiirc.org (accessed 1 July 2013).

Ismail, M. (2009). Corporate Social Responsibility and its Role in Community Development: An International Perspective. *Journal of International Social Research*, 2(9), 199–209.

Jacobs, M. (1991). Sustainable Development, Capital Substitution and Economic Humility: A Response to Beckerman. *Environmental Values*, 4(1), 57–68.

Jahn, T. and Keil, F. (2006). Transdisziplinärer Forschungsprozess. In Becker, E. and Jahn, T. (eds), *Soziale Ökologie: Grundzüge einer Wissenschaft von den gesellschaftlichen Naturverhältnissen.* Frankfurt am Main: Campus-Verlag, 319–29.

Jamali, D. and Mirshak, R. (2007). Corporate Social Responsibility (CSR) Theory and Practice in a Developing Country Context. *Journal of Business Ethics*, 72, 243–62.

Johnson, R.B. and Onwuegbuzie, A.J. (2004). Mixed Methods Research: A Research Paradigm whose Time Has Come. *Educational Researcher*, 33(7), 14–26.

Jones, R.A. (1986). *Emile Durkheim: An Introduction to Four Major Works.* Beverly Hills, CA: Sage, 60–81.

Jonker, J. and Nijhof, A. (2006). Looking through the Eyes of Others: Assessing Mutual Expectations and Experiences in Order to Shape Dialogue and Collaboration Between Business and NGOs with Respect to CSR. *Corporate Governance: An International Review*, 14(5), 456–66.

Juholin, E. (2004). For Business or the Good of All? A Finnish Approach to Corporate Social Responsibility. *Corporate Governance*, 4(3), 20–31.

Karoly, K. (2013). The Rise and Fall of the Concept of Sustainability. *Journal of Environmental Sustainability*, 1(1), 1–12.

Khan, A. (1995). Sustainable Development: The Key Concepts, Issues and Implications. *Sustainable Development*, 3, 63–9.

Kinderman, D. (2010). The Political Economy of Corporate Responsibility Across Europe and Beyond: 1977–2007. PhD diss.: Cornell University.

—— (2011). "Free Us Up So We Can Be Responsible!" The Co-Evolution of Corporate Social Responsibility and Neo-Liberalisms in the UK, 1977–2010. *Socio-Economic Review*, 10(1), 1–29.

Kinderyte, L. (2008). Analysis and Comparison of Methodologies for Corporate Sustainability Assessment. *Environmental Research Engineering and Management*, 4(46), 66–75.

King, A. (2002). How to Get Started in Corporate Social Responsibility. *Financial Management* (October), 5.

Klein, J.T. (2008). Evaluation of Interdisciplinary and Transdisciplinary Research: A Literature Review. *American Journal of Preventive Medicine*, 35(2), S116–S123.

Kotler, P. and Lee, N. (2005). *Corporate Social Responsibility: Doing the Most Good for Your Company and Your Cause*. Hoboken, NJ: Wiley.

Kramer, R.M. (1999). Trust and Distrust in Organizations: Emerging Perspectives, Enduring Questions. *Annual Review of Psychology*, 50(1), 569–98.

Kuhlman, T. and Farrington, J. (2010). What is Sustainability? *Sustainability*, 2(11), 3436–48.

Kumar, M. and Kumar, P. (2007). Valuation of the Ecosystem Services: A Psycho-Cultural Perspective. *Ecological Economics*, 64, 808–19.

Lafferty, W. and Meadowcroft, J. (eds) (2000). *Implementing Sustainable Development*. Oxford: Oxford University Press.

Lang, D.J., Wiek, A., Bergmann, M., Stauffacher, M., Martens, P., Moll, P., Swilling, M. and Thomas, C.J. (2012). Transdisciplinary Research in Sustainability Science: Practice, Principles, and Challenges. *Sustainability Science*, 7(supp. 1), 25–43.

Lechat, B. (2012). For a Green Reconquest of Equality. In Lechat, B. (ed.), *Green European Journal*, 4 (December): Equality and Sustainability, 3–7.

Lele, S. (1991). Some Comments on Coordinate Free and Scale Invariant Methods in Morphometrics. *American Journal of Physical Anthropology*, 85, 405–18.

Lépineux, F. (2003). Dans quelle mesure une entreprise peut-elle être responsable à l'égard de la cohésion sociale? PhD diss.: Conservatoire National des Arts et Métiers.

Levitt, T. (1958). The Dangers of Social Responsibly. *Harvard Business Review*, (September–October), 41–50.

Littig, B. and Grießier, E. (2005). Social Sustainability: A Catchword between Political Pragmatism and Social Theory. *International Journal of Sustainable Development*, 8(1/2), 65–79.

Longo, M., Mura, M. and Bonoli, A. (2005). Corporate Social Responsibility and Corporate Performance: The Case of Italian SMEs. *Corporate Governance*, 5(4), 28–42.

Lopez, M.V., Garcia, A. and Rodriguez, L. (2007). Sustainable Development and Corporate Performance: A Study Based on the Dow Jones Sustainability Index. *Journal of Business Ethics*, 75, 285–300.

Loranzo, J.M. (2005). *Governments and Corporate Social Responsibility. Publication, Politics, Regulations and Voluntariness*. Barcelona: Doubleday.

Luhmann, N. (1981). *Soziologische Aufklarung*, vol. 3. Opladen: Westdeutscher Verlag.

Luo, J.D. (2005). Particularistic Trust and General Trust: A Network Analysis in Chinese Organizations. *Management and Organizational Review*, 1(3), 437–58.

McKenzie, S. (2004). *Social Sustainability: Towards Some Definitions*. Hawke Research Institute Working Paper Series, No. 27.

Mackey, J. and Sisodia, R. (2014). *Conscious Capitalism: Liberating the Heroic Spirit of Business*. Boston, MA: Harvard Business Review Press.

McNamee, S. (1994). Research as Relationally Situated Activity: Ethical Implications. *Journal of Feminist Family Therapy*, 6(3), 69–83.

—— (1996). Therapy and Identity Construction in a Postmodern World. In Grodin, D. and Lindlof, T.R. (eds), *Constructing the Self in a Mediated World*. London: Sage, 141–55.

—— and Gergen, K.J. (1999). *Relational Responsibility: Resources for Sustainable Dialogue*. Thousand Oaks: Sage.

McWilliams, A. and Siegel, D.S. (2000). Corporate Social Responsibility and Financial Performance: Correlation or Misspecification? *Strategic Management Journal*, 21(5), 603–9.

—— and Wright, P.M. (2006). Corporate Social Responsibility: Strategic Implications. *Journal of Management Studies*, 43(1), 1–18.

——, Van Fleet, D.D. and Cory, K. (2002). Raising Rivals Costs through Political Strategy: An Extension of the Resource-Based Theory. *Journal of Management Studies*, 39, 707–23.

Magis, K. and Shinn, C. (2009). Emergent Themes of Social Sustainability. In Dillard, J., Dijon, V. and King, M.C. (eds), *Understanding the Social Aspect of Sustainability*. New York: Routledge, 15–44.

Maignan, I. and Ralston, D.A. (2002). Corporate Social Responsibility in Europe and the US: Insights from Businesses' Self Presentations. *Journal of International Business Studies*, 33, 497–514.

Makower, J. (1994). *Beyond the Bottom Line*. London: Simon & Schuster.

Marcus, A.A. and Anderson, M.H. (2006). A General Dynamic Capability: Does it Propagate Business and Social Competencies in the Retail Food Industry? *Journal of Management Studies*, 43(1), 19–46.

Margolis, J.D. and Walsh, J.P. (2001). *People and Profits? The Search for a Link between a Company's Social and Financial Performance*. Mahwah, NJ: Lawrence Erlbaum.

Marquis, C., Glynnn, M.A. and Davis, G.F. (2007). Community Isomorphism and Corporate Social Action. *Academy of Management Review*, 32(3), 799–820.

Matten, D. and Crane, A. (2005). Corporate Citizenship: Towards an Extended Theoretical Conceptualization. *Academy of Management Review*, 30(1), 166–79.

—— and Moon, J. (2008). "Implicit" And "Explicit" CSR: A Conceptual Framework for a Comparative Understanding of Corporate Social Responsibility. *Academy of Management Review*, 33(2), 404–24.

——, Crane, A. and Chapple, W. (2003). Behind the Mask: Revealing the True Face of Corporate Citizenship. *Journal of Business Ethics*, 45(1/2), 109–14.

Mayer, A.L. (2007). Strengths and Weaknesses of Common Sustainability Indices for Multidimensional Systems. *Environment International*, 34, 277–91.

Meadowcroft, J. (1999). Planning for Sustainable Development: What can be Learned from the Critics? In Kenny, M. and Meadowcroft, J. (eds), *Planning Sustainability*. New York: Routledge, 12–40.

Melhus, P. and Paton, B. (2013). The Paradox of Multi-Stakeholder Collaborations: Insights from Sustainable Silicon Valley's Regional CO2 Emissions Reduction Program. *Journal of Environmental Sustainability*, 2(2), 29–44.

Mersereau, A. and Mottis, N. (2011). *Corporate Social Responsibility and Management Control*. Research Center ESSEC Working Paper 1114.

Meznar, M.B., Chrisman, J.J. and Carroll, A.B. (1990). *Social Responsibility and Strategic Management: Toward an Enterprise Strategy Classification*. Paper presented at the National Academy of Management meetings. San Francisco.

Mihelcic, J.R., Crittenden, J.C., Small, M.J., Shonnard, D.R., Hokanson, D.R., Zhang, Q., Chen, H., Sorby, S.A., James, V.U., Sutherland, J.W. and Schnoor, J.L. (2003). Sustainability Science and Engineering: The Emergence of a New Metadiscipline. *Environmental Science Technology*, 37, 5314–24.

Moon, J. (2004). *Government as a Driver of Corporate Social Responsibility*. No. 20-2004 ICCSR Research Paper Series—ISSN 1479-512. Available at: http://www.nottingham.ac.uk/business/ICCSR (accessed 12 September 2009).

—— and Vogel, D. (2008). Corporate Responsibility, Government and Civil Society. In Crane, A., McWilliams, A., Matten D., Moon, J. and Siegel, D. (eds), *Oxford Handbook of Corporate Social Responsibility*. Oxford: Oxford University Press, 303–26.

Newell, P. (2005). Citizenship, Accountability and Community: The Limits of the CSR Agenda. *International Affairs*, 81(3), 541–57.

Newig, J., Pahl-Wostl, C. and Sigel, K. (2005). The Role of Public Participation in Managing Uncertainty in the Implementation of the Water Directive. *European Environment*, 15, 333–43.

Nolan, P., Shipman, A. and Rui, H. (2004). Coal Liquefaction, Shenhua Group and China's Energy Security. *European Management Journal*, 22(2), 150–64.

Noren, G. (2004). *The Role of Business in Society*. Stockholm: Confederation of Swedish Enterprise.

Norgaard, R.B. (1994). *Development Betrayed: The End of Progress and a Coevolutionary Revisioning of the Future*. New York: Routledge.

Norton, B.G. (2005). *Sustainability: A Philosophy of Adaptive Ecosystem Management*. Chicago: University of Chicago Press.

OECD (2013). *Measuring Well-Being for Development.* Discussion Paper for Session 3.1. Available at: www.oecd.org/site/oecdgfd/ (accessed 1 November 2013).

Okin, S.M. (1999). Is Multiculturalism Bad for Women? In Cohen, J., Howard, M. and Nussbaum, M.C. (eds), *Is Multiculturalism Bad for Women?* Princeton, NJ: Princeton University Press.

Olmix (n.d.). *Sustainable Development.* Available at: www.olmix.com (accessed 1 March 2013).

Othman, A. and Abdellatif, M. (2011). Partnership for Integrating the Corporate Social Responsibility of Project Stakeholders towards Affordable Housing Development. *Journal of Engineering, Design and Technology,* 9(3), 273–95.

Opp, S.M. and Saunders, K.L. (2013). Pillar Talk: Local Sustainability Initiatives and policies in the United States-Finding Evidence of the "Three E's": Economic Development, Environmental Protection, and Social Equity. *Urban Affairs Review,* 20(10), 1–40.

Orlitzky, M., Schmidt, F.L. and Rynes, S.L. (2003). Corporate Social and Financial Performance: A Meta-Analysis. *Organizational Studies,* 24(3), 403–41.

O'Toole, R. (2013). Reducing Livability: How Sustainability Planning Threatens the American Dream. *Cato Institute Policy Analysis,* 740, 1–22.

Owen, D. (2008). Chronicles of Wasted Time? A Personal Reflection on the Current State of, and Future Prospects for, Social and Environmental Accounting Research. *Accounting, Auditing, and Accountability Journal,* 21(2), 240–67.

Pajares, F. (2002). *Overview of Social Cognitive Theory and of Self-Efficacy.* Available at: http://www/emory.edu/EDUCATION/mpf/eff.html (accessed 14 September 2013).

Parris, T.M. and Kates, R.W. (2003). Characterizing and Measuring Sustainable Development. *Annual Review Environmental Resource,* 28(13), 13–28.

Pater, A. and van Lierop, K. (2006). Sense and Sensitivity: The Roles of Organization and Stakeholders in Managing Corporate Social Responsibility. *Business Ethics: A European Review*, 15(4), 339–51.

Pawel, U. (2009). Competitiveness and Company Motives for Pro-ethical Actions: Slovak Students' Opinions. *Journal of Competitiveness*. Available at: www.cjournal.cz/files/4.pdf (accessed 12 September 2013).

Peachey, D.E. and Lerner, M.J. (1981). Law as a Social Trap: Problems and Possibilities for the Future. In Lerner, M.J. and Lerner, S.C. (eds), *The Justice Motive in Social Behavior: Adapting to Times of Scarcity and Change*. New York: Plenum Press.

Pearce, W.B. and Pearce, K.A. (2000). Extending the Theory of the Coordinated Management of Meaning (CMM) through a Community Dialogue Process. *Communication Theory*, 10(4), 405–23.

Petkoski, D. and Twose, N. (eds) (2003). *Public Policy for Corporate Social Responsibility*. WBI Series on Corporate Responsibility, Accountability, and Sustainable Competitiveness.

Phillips, R.A. (1997). Stakeholder Theory and a Principle of Fairness. *Business Ethics Quarterly*, 7(1), 51–66.

Picone, P.M., Dagnino, G.B. and Mina, A. (2014). The Origin of Failure: A Multidisciplinary Appraisal of the Hubris Hypothesis and Proposed Research Agenda. *Academy of Management Perspectives*, 28(4), 447–68.

Pini, B. (2004). On Being a Nice Country Girl and an Academic Feminist: Using Reflexivity in Rural Social Research. *Journal of Rural Studies*, 20, 169–79.

Pohl, C. (2008). From Science to Policy through Transdisciplinary Research. *Environmental Science and Policy*, 11, 46–53.

Polanyi, K. (2001). *The Great Transformation: The Political and Economic Origins of Our Time*. Boston, MA: Beacon Press.

Porter, M.E. and Kramer, M.R. (2006). Strategy and Society: The Link between Competitive Advantage and Corporate Social Responsibility. *Harvard Business Review*, 84(12), 78–92.

—— (2011). Creating Shared Value. *Harvard Business Review* (January). Available at: http://hbr.org (accessed 8 October 2014).

——, Stern, S. and Artavia Loria, R. (2013). *Social Progress Index*. Available at: www.socialprogressimperative.org (accessed 8 October 2014).

Prahalad, C.K. and Hamel, G. (1994). Strategy as a Field of Study: Why Search for a New Paradigm? *Strategic Management Journal*, 15, 5–16.

Prescott-Allen, R. (2001). *The Wellbeing of Nations: A Country-by-Country Index of Quality of Life and the Environment*. Washington, DC: Island Press.

Preston, L.E. and Post, J.E. (1975). *Private Management and Public Policy: The Principle of Public Responsibility*. Englewood-Cliffs, NJ: Prentice Hall.

—— and Sapienza, H.T. (1990). Stakeholder Management and Corporate Performance. *Journal of Behavioral Economics*, 1(9), 361–75.

Prieto-Carron, M., Lund-Thomsen, P., Chan, A. and Bhushan, C. (2006). Critical Perspectives on CSR and Development: What we Know, What We Don't Know, and What We Need to Know. *International Affairs*, 82(5), 977–87.

Procter & Gamble (2012). *Sustainability Report*. Available at: www.pg.com (accessed 1 March 2013).

Protocan, V. and Mulej, M. (2009). How to Improve Innovativeness of Small and Medium Enterprises. *Management*, 14(1), 1–20.

Quazi, A. and O'Brien, D. (2000). An Empirical Test of a Cross-National Model of Corporate Social Responsibility. *Journal of Business Ethics*, 25, 33–51.

Raffaelle, R., Robinson, W. and Selinger, E. (2010). *Sustainability Ethics*. New York: Automatic Press.

Ratiu, C. and Anderson, B.B. (2014). The Identity Crisis of Sustainable Development. *World Journal of Science, Technology and Sustainable Development*, 11(1), 4–15.

Redclift, M. (1999). Sustainability and Markets: On the Neo-Classical Model of Environmental Economics. In Kenny, M. and Meadowcroft, J. (eds), *Planning Sustainability*. New York: Routledge, 66–77.

Reihlen, M. and Ringberg, T. (2013). Uncertainty, Pluralism, and the Knowledge-Based Theory of the Firm: From J.-C. Spender's Contribution to a Socio-Cognitive Approach. *European Management Journal*, 31(6), 706–16.

Reinhardt, E.L. (1998). Environmental Product Differentiation: Implications for Corporate Strategy. *California Management Review*, 40, 43–73.

Robinson, J. (2008). Being Undisciplined: Transgressions and Intersections in Academia and Beyond. *Futures*, 40, 70–86.

Rosanvallon, P. (2012). Rethinking Equality in an Age of Inequalities. In Lechat, B. (ed.), *Green European Journal*, 4 (December): Equality and Sustainability, 8–14.

Rousseau, D.M., Sitkin, S.B., Burt, R.S. and Camerer, C. (1998). Not So Different After All: A Cross-Discipline View of Trust. *Academy of Management Review*, 23(3), 393–401.

Ruf, B., Muralidhar, K., Brown, R., Janney, J. and Paul, K. (2001). An Empirical Investigation of the Relationship between Change in Corporate Social Performance and Financial Performance: A Stakeholder Theory Perspective. *Journal of Business Ethics*, 32(2), 143–56.

Saisana, M. and Philippas, D. (2012). *Sustainable Society Index (SSI): Taking Societies' Pulse along the Social, Environmental and Economic Issues. European Commission, JRC Scientific and Policy Reports, Joint Research Centre Audit on the SSI*. Available at: www.ssfindex.com/cms/wp-content/…/JRCauditSSI2006_2012.pdf (accessed 1 May 2013).

Sasse, C.M. and Trahan, R.T. (2007). Rethinking the New Corporate Philanthropy. *Business Horizons*, 50(1), 29–38.

Schaltegger, S. (2012). *Sustainability Reporting in the Light of Business Environments. Linking Business Environment, Strategy, Communication and Accounting.* Leuphana University Centre for Sustainability Management, Discussion Paper, March 2012.

—— and Ludeke-Freund, F. (2012). *The "Business Case for Sustainability" Concept: A Short Introduction.* Lüneburg: Leuphana University Centre for Sustainability Management.

Schein, E.H. (1985). *Organizational Culture and Leadership.* San Francisco: Jossey-Bass.

Schwartz, M.S. and Carroll, A.B. (2003). Corporate Social Responsibility: A Three-Domain Approach. *Business Ethics Quarterly,* 13(4), 503–30.

Scott, M. (2004). Corporate Social Responsibility: A Burning Issue for Recruits. *Financial Times* (18 October). Available at: www.ft.com (accessed 1 May 2013).

—— and Rothman, H. (1992). *Companies with a Conscience: Intimate Portraits of Twelve Firms that Make a Difference.* New York: Citadel.

Scruggs, C.E. and Buren, H.J. III (2014). Why Leading Consumer Companies Develop Proactive Chemical Management Strategies. *Business and Society* (22 June), 1–41. Available at: http://bas.sagepub.com/content/early/2014/06/21/0007650314536393 (accessed 5 September 2014).

Seager, T., Sellinger, E. and Wiek, A. (2011). Sustainable Engineering Science for Resolving Wicked Problems. *Journal of Agricultural Environmental Ethics,* 25(4), 467–84.

Selman, P. (1999). Three Decades of Environmental Planning: What Have We Really Learned? In Kenny, M. and Meadowcroft, J. (eds), *Planning Sustainability.* New York: Routledge, 148–74.

Shamir, R. (2005). Mind the Gap: The Commodification of Corporate Social Responsibility. *Symbolic Interaction,* 28, 229–53.

—— (2010). Capitalism, Governance, and Authority: The Case of Corporate Social Responsibility. *Annual Review of Law and Social Science*, 6, 531–53.

Shared Value Initiative (2014). *Banking on Shared Value. How Banks Profit by Rethinking Their Purpose*. Available at: www.fsg.org (accessed 5 September 2014).

Snieska, V. and Bruneckiene, J. (2009). Measurement of Lithuanian Regions by Regional Competiveness Index. *Engineering Economics*, 1(61), 45–57.

Social Impact Investment Taskforce (2014a). *Lessons from the Social Impact Investment Taskforce*. Available at: www.giin.org (accessed 21 December 2014).

—— (2014b). *Measuring Impact*. Available at: www.socialimpactinvestment. org/reports/Measuring%20Impact%20WG%20paper%20FINAL.pdf (accessed 1 October 2014).

Spangenberg, J.H. (1997). Environmental Space-Based Proactive Linkage Indicators: A Compass on the Road Towards Sustainability. In Moldan, B. and Billharz, S. (eds), *Sustainability Indicators, Report of the Project on Indicators of Sustainable Development*. London: Wiley.

Spector, B. (2008). Business Responsibilities in a Divided World: The Cold War Roots of the Corporate Social Responsibility Movement. *Enterprise and Society*, 9, 314–36.

Stanford, C.B. (2001). The Ape's Gift: Meat-Eating, Meat-Sharing, and Human Evolution. In De Waal, F.B.M. (ed.), *Tree of Origin: What Primate Behavior Can Tell Us about Human Social Evolution*. Cambridge, MA: Harvard University Press.

Stern, S., Wares, A., Orzell, S. and O'Sullivan, P. (2014). *Social Progress Index 2014: Methodological Report*. Available at: www.socialprogressimperative. org (accessed 8 October 2014).

Steurer, R. (2010). The Role of Governments in Corporate Social Responsibility: Characterising Public Policies on CSR in Europe. *Policy Sciences*, 43(1), 49–72.

——, Margula, S. and Martinuzzi, A. (2012). *Public Policies on CSR in Europe: Themes, Instruments, and Regional Differences.* InFER Discussion Paper 2-2012. Available at: http://ssrn.com/abstract=2342149 (accessed 27 December 2014).

Storper, M. (1997). Territories, Flows and Hierarchies in the Global Economy. In Cox, K.R. (ed.), *Spaces of Globalization: Reasserting the Power of the Local.* New York: Guilford Press, 19–44.

Swanson, D.L. (1995). Addressing a Theoretical Problem by Reorienting the Corporate Social Performance Model. *Academy of Management Review,* 20(1), 43–64.

Swift, T. (2001). Trust, Reputation and Corporate Accountability to Stakeholders. *Business Ethics: A European Review,* 10(1), 16–26.

Thiel, M. (2010). Innovations in Corporate Social Responsibility from Global Business Leaders at Panasonic, Thomson Reuters and Nanyang Business School. *American Journal of Economics and Business Administration,* 2(2), 1–8.

—— (2013). Review of Patrick Kilby, NGOs in India: The Challenges of Women's Empowerment and Accountability. *South Asian Journal of Global Business Research,* 2(1), 149–52.

Thompson, B., Teeuwen, E. and Georgieva, I. (2014). The Legal Aspects of Corporate Social Responsibility: Interview with Ursula Wynhoven. *Utrecht Journal of International and European Law,* 30(78), 139–44. Available at: http://dx.doi.org/10.5334/ujiel.ch (accessed 27 December 2014).

Tornatzky, L.G. and Klein, K. (1982). Innovation Characteristics and Innovation Adoption-Implementation: A Meta-Analysis of Findings. *IEEE Transactions on Engineering Management,* 29(1), 28–43.

Tumay, M. (2009). Why Corporate Social Responsibility: A New Concept in the 21st Century. *Journal of Economics,* 16(2), 63–72.

Turner, B.L., Kasperson, R.E., Matson, P.A., McCarthy, J.J., Corell, R.W., Christensen, L., Eckley, N., Kasperson, J.X., Luers, A., Martello, M.L., Polsky, C., Pulsipher, A. and Schiller, A. (2003). A Framework for Vulnerability Analysis in Sustainability Science. *Proceedings of the National Academy of Sciences*, 100(14), 8074–79.

Uddin, M.B., Hassan, M.R. and Tarique, K.M. (2008). Three Dimensional Aspects of Corporate Social Responsibility. *Daffodil: International University Journal of Business and Economics*, 3(1), 199–212.

Uhlaner, L., Van Goor-Balk, A. and Masurel, E. (2004). Family Business and Corporate Social Responsibility in a Sample of Dutch Firms. *Journal of Small Business and Enterprise Development*, 1(2), 186–94.

Ullmann, A. (1985). Data in Search of a Theory: A Critical Examination of the Relationship among Social Performance, Social Disclosure, and Economic Performance. *Academy of Management Review*, 10, 450–77.

Ulrich, P. (2008). Corporate Citizenship oder: Das politische Moment guter Unternehmensführung in der Bürgergesellschaft. In Backhaus-Maul, H., Biedermann, C., Nährlich, S. and Polterauer, J. (eds), *Corporate Citizenship in Deutschland: Bilanz und Perspektiven*. Wiesbaden: Verlag für Sozialwissenschaft, 94–100.

UNDP [United Nations Development Program] (2004). *Human Development Report. Cultural Liberty in Today's Diverse World*. Available at: http://hdr.undp.org (accessed 1 May 2013).

Uslaner, E.M. and Conley, R.S. (2003). Civic Engagement and Particularized Trust: The Ties that Bind People to their Ethnic Communities. *American Politics Research*, 31(4), 331–60.

Valor, C. (2005). Corporate Social Responsibility and Corporate Citizenship: Towards Corporate Accountability. *Business and Society Review*, 110(2), 191–212.

Van Beurden, P. and Gossling, T. (2008). The Worth of Values: A Literature Review on the Relation Between Corporate Social and Financial Performance. *Journal of Business Ethics*, 82, 407–24.

Van Knippenberg, A.F.M. (1984). Intergroup Difference in Group Perceptions. In Tajfel, H. (ed). *The Social Dimension: European Developments in Social Psychology*. Cambridge: Cambridge University Press.

Van Marrewijk, M. and Were, M. (2003). Multiple Levels of Corporate Sustainability. *Journal of Business Ethics*, 44(2/3), 107–19.

Votaw, D. and Prakash, S.S. (1973). *The Corporate Dilemma: Traditional Values versus Contemporary Problems*. Englewood Cliffs, NJ: Prentice Hall.

Waddock, S.A. and Graves, S.B. (1997). The Corporate Social Performance Financial Performance Link. *Strategic Management Journal*, 18(4), 303–19.

Waldman, D.A., Sully de Luque, M., Washburn, N. and House, R.J. (2006). Cultural and Leadership Predictors of Corporate Social Responsibility Values of Top Management: A Global Study of 15 Countries. *Journal of International Business Studies*, 37(6), 823–37.

Wartick, S.L. and Cochran, P.L. (1985). The Evolution of the Corporate Social Performance Model. *Academy of Management Review*, 10(4), 758–69.

—— and Wood, D.J. (1998). *International Business and Society*. Malden: Blackwell.

Weick, K.E. (1987). Organizational Culture as a Source of High Reliability. *California Management Review*, 29(2), 112–27.

Weterings, R. and Opschoor, J. (1994). Environmental Utilization Space and Reference Values for Performance Evaluation. *Milieu*, 9, 221–8.

Wiek, A., Farioli, F., Fukushi, K. and Yarime, M. (2012a). Sustainability Science: Bridging the Gap between Science and Society. *Sustainability Science*, 7(supp. 1), 1–4.

——, Ness, B., Schweizer-Ries, P., Brand, F.S. and Farioli, F. (2012b). From Complex Systems Analysis to Transformational Change: A Comparative Appraisal of Sustainability Science Projects. *Sustainability Science*, 7(supp. 1), 5–24.

Wiersum, K. Freerk (1995). 200 Years of Sustainability in Forestry: Lessons from History. *Environmental Management*, 19(3), 321–9.

Williams, C.A. and Aguilera, R.A. (2008). Corporate Social Responsibility in a Comparative Perspective. In Crane, A., McWilliams, A., Matten, D., Moon, J. and Siegel, D.S. (eds), *The Oxford Handbook of Corporate Social Responsibility*. New York: Oxford University Press.

Windsor, D. (2001). The Future of Corporate Social Responsibility. *International Journal of Organizational Analysis*, 9(3), 225–56.

Wise, S. (2014). Can a Team Have Too Much Cohesion? The Dark Side to Network Density. *European Management Journal*, 32(5), 703–11.

Wood, D.J. (1991). Corporate Social Performance Revisited. *Academy of Management Review*, 16(4), 691–718.

—— and Jones, R.E. (1995). Stakeholder Mismatching: A Theoretical Problem in Empirical Research on Corporate Social Performance. *International Journal of Organizational Analysis*, 3, 229–67.

World Bank Development Report (2015). *Mind, Society and Behavior*. Available at: www.worldbank.org (accessed 21 December 2014).

Index

For Product Safety Concerns and Information please contact our EU
representative GPSR@taylorandfrancis.com Taylor & Francis Verlag GmbH,
Kaufingerstraße 24, 80331 München, Germany

Printed and bound by CPI Group (UK) Ltd, Croydon, CR0 4YY
01/05/2025
01858452-0007